CLASSIC SERMONS ON HEAVEN AND HELL

KREGEL CLASSIC SERMONS Series

Classic Sermons on the Attributes of God

Classic Sermons on the Birth of Christ

Classic Sermons on Christian Service

Classic Sermons on the Cross of Christ

Classic Sermons on Faith and Doubt

Classic Sermons on Family and Home

Classic Sermons on Heaven and Hell

Classic Sermons on Hope

Classic Sermons on the Names of God

Classic Sermons on Overcoming Fear

Classic Sermons on Praise

Classic Sermons on Prayer

Classic Sermons on the Prodigal Son

Classic Sermons on the Resurrection of Christ

Classic Sermons on the Second Coming and Other Prophetic Themes

Classic Sermons on the Sovereignty of God

Classic Sermons on Spiritual Warfare

Classic Sermons on Suffering

Classic Sermons on Worship

KREGEL CLASSIC SERMONS SERIES

CLASSIC SERMONS ON HEAVEN AND HELL

Compiled by
Warren W. Wiersbe

kregel
PUBLICATIONS

Grand Rapids, MI 49501

Classic Sermons on Heaven and Hell,
compiled by Warren W. Wiersbe.

Copyright © 1994 by Kregel Publications. All rights reserved. No part of this book may be reproduced, stored in a retrieval system, or transmitted in any form or by any means—electronic, mechanical, photocopy, recording, or otherwise—without written permission of the publisher, except for brief quotations in printed reviews.

Published by Kregel Publications, a division of Kregel, Inc., P.O. Box 2607, Grand Rapids, MI 49501. Kregel Publications provides trusted, biblical publications for Christian growth and service. Your comments and suggestions are valued.

Cover photo: INTERNATIONAL STOCK/Warren Faidley
Cover and Book Design: Alan G. Hartman

Library of Congress Cataloging-in-Publication Data

Classic sermons on heaven and hell / compiled by Warren W. Wiersbe.
    p.   cm.— (Kregel classic sermons series)
  Includes index.
  1. Heaven—Sermons. 2. Hell—Sermons. 3. Sermons, English. I. Wiersbe, Warren W. II. Series: Kregel classic sermons series.
BT846.2.C53   1994   236'.24—dc20   94-3746
                                                                           CIP
ISBN   0-8254-3995-7 (pbk.)

1 2 3 4 5 Printing / Year 98 97 96 95 94

Printed in the United States of America

CONTENTS

List of Scripture Texts 6
Preface 7

1. Heaven 9
   Dwight Lyman Moody
2. What Will the Faithful Do in Heaven? 23
   Henry H. Savage
3. Heaven 35
   John Charles Ryle
4. The Homesickness of the Soul 47
   William E. Sangster
5. The Heavenly Home 57
   John Ker
6. The Door to Heaven 73
   George W. Truett
7. Many Mansions 85
   Alexander Maclaren
8. A Glimpse of the Afterlife 95
   Clovis Gillham Chappell
9. The Barrier 107
   Charles Haddon Spurgeon
10. Future Punishment Eternal 127
    Robert Murray McCheyne
11. The Eternity of Hell Torments 137
    Jonathan Edwards

LIST OF SCRIPTURE TEXTS

Luke 11:2, Moody 9
Luke 19:12–19, Savage 23
Revelation 21:27, Ryle 35
2 Corinthians 5:8, Sangster 47
John 14:2, Ker 57
Revelation 4:1, Truett 73
John 14:2, Maclaren 85
Luke 16:23, Chappell 95
Revelation 21:27, Spurgeon 107
Mark 9:44, McCheyne 127
Matthew 25:46, Edwards 137

PREFACE

THE *KREGEL CLASSIC SERMONS SERIES* is an attempt to assemble and publish meaningful sermons from master preachers about significant themes.

These are *sermons*, not essays or chapters taken from books about themes. Not all of these sermons could be called "great," but all of them are *meaningful*. They apply the truths of the Bible to the needs of the human heart, which is something that all effective preaching must do.

While some are better known than others, all of the preachers whose sermons I have selected had important ministries and were highly respected in their day. The fact that a sermon is included in this volume does not mean that either the compiler or the publisher agrees with or endorses everything that the man did, preached, or wrote. The sermon is here because it has a valued contribution to make.

These are sermons about *significant* themes. The pulpit is no place to play with trivia. The preacher has thirty minutes in which to help mend broken hearts, change defeated lives, and save lost souls; and he can never accomplish this demanding ministry by distributing homiletical tidbits. In these difficult days we do not need "clever" pulpiteers who discuss the times; we need dedicated ambassadors who will preach the eternities.

The reading of these sermons can enrich your spiritual life. The studying of them can enrich your skills as an interpreter and expounder of God's truth. However God uses these sermons in your life and ministry, my prayer is that His Church around the world will be encouraged and strengthened by them.

WARREN W. WIERSBE

Heaven

Dwight Lyman Moody (1837–1899) is known around the world as one of America's most effective evangelists. Converted as a teenager through the witness of his Sunday school teacher, Moody became active in YMCA and Sunday school work in Chicago while pursuing a successful business career. He then devoted his full time to evangelism and was used mightily of God in campaigns in both the United States and Great Britain. He founded the Northfield School for girls, the Mount Hermon School for boys, the Northfield Bible Conference, and the Moody Bible Institute in Chicago. Before the days of planes and radio, Moody traveled more than a million miles and addressed more than one hundred million people.

This message is from *The Gospel Awakening*, edited by L. T. Remlap (Chicago: J. Fairbanks & Co., 1879).

Dwight Lyman Moody

1

HEAVEN

Our Father, which art in heaven (Luke 11:2).

WE HAVE FOR our subject this evening, heaven. It is not as some talk about heaven, as just the air. I find a good many people now that think there is no heaven, only just here in this world; that this is all the heaven we will ever see. I talked with a man the other day, who said he thought there is nothing to justify us in believing there is any other heaven than that which we are in now. Well, if this is heaven, it is a very strange kind of heaven—this world of sickness, and sorrow, and sin. If he thinks this is really all the heaven we are going to see, he has a queer idea of it. There are three heavens spoken of in the Bible, and the Hebrews acknowledge in their writings three heavens. The first is the aerial—the air, the wind, the air that the birds fly in; that is one heaven. Then, there is the heaven of the firmament, where the stars are; and then there is the heaven of heavens, where God's throne is and the mansions of the Lord are—the mansions of light and peace, the home of the blessed, the home of the Redeemer, where the angels dwell. That is the heaven that we believe in, and the heaven that we want to talk about today. We believe it is just as much a place and just as much a city as New York is, and a good deal more; because New York will pass away, and that city will abide forever. It has foundations, whose builder and maker is God. I do not think it is wrong for us to speculate, and think about, and talk about heaven. I was going to a meeting once, some time ago, when I was asked by a friend on the way, "What will be the subject of your speech?" I said, "My subject will be heaven." He scowled, and I asked, "Why do you look so?" He said: "I was in hopes you would give us something practical tonight. We cannot know anything about heaven. It is all speculation." Now, all

Scripture is given us by the inspiration of God. Some is given for warnings, some for encouragement. If God did not want us to think about heaven and talk about it down here, there would not be so much said about heaven in Scripture. There would not be so many promises about it. If we thought more about those mansions God is preparing for us, we would be thinking more of things above, and less of things of this earth.

God Dwells in Heaven

I like to locate heaven, and find out all about it I can. I expect to live there through eternity. If I was going to dwell in any place in this country, if I was going to make it my home, I would want to inquire all about the place, about its climate, about what kind of neighbors I was going to have, about the schools for my children, about everything, in fact, that I could learn concerning it. If any of you who are here were going to emigrate, going off to some other country, and I was going to take that for my subject tonight, why, would not all your ears be open to hear what you could learn about it? Would you then be looking around to see who was sitting next you; and who among your acquaintances were here; and what people were thinking about you? You would be all interested in hearing of this country that I was talking about. You could not think anything about the latest fashion, or about some woman's hairstyle. If it is true that we are going to spend eternity in another world, and that God is inviting us to spend it with Him, shall we not look and listen, and find out where He is, and who is there, and how we are to get there? Soon after I was converted, an infidel got hold of me one day, and he asked me why I looked up when I prayed. He said that heaven was no more above us than below us, that heaven was everywhere. Well, I was greatly bewildered, and the next time I prayed it did seem as though I was praying into the air. His words had sowed the seed. Since then I have not only become better acquainted with the Bible, but I have come to see that heaven is above us; it is upward. If you will turn to the seventeenth chapter of Genesis, you will see that it says that God went up from Abraham. In the third chapter of John, in the wonderful conversation that Christ had with Nicodemus, He told him that He came down from heaven; and as we read in the first chapter of Acts, "They saw him go up into heaven"—not down—"and the clouds received him out of their sight." If you will turn to 1 Kings 8:30, I will show you that God has a dwelling place. A great many people have gone upon their reason until they have reasoned away God. They say God is not a person that we can ever see. He is the God of nature. "And hearken thou to the supplication of thy servant, and of thy people Israel, when they shall pray toward this place; and hear thou in heaven, thy dwelling place, and when thou hearest, forgive." Some people are trying to find out and wonder how far heaven is away. There is one thing we know about that: it is that it is not so far away but that God can hear us when we pray. There is not a sigh goes up to Him but that He hears it. He hears His children when they cry. God has a throne and a dwelling place in heaven. In 2 Chronicles 7:14 it says, "If my people which are called by my name shall humble themselves, and pray and seek my face and turn from their wicked ways, then will I hear from heaven, and will forgive their sin, and will heal their land."

There are a good many promises given us to encourage us to pray, and to teach us that God hears us when we do pray; that He is not so far away but that He hears us. When Christ was on earth, they came to Him and said, "Teach us how to pray to our heavenly Father." He taught them a prayer. It began, "Our Father which art"—not on earth—no; but, "Our Father which art in heaven." Now, when we go to heaven we will be with our Father Himself. If you will turn to Acts 7:55 it says, "But he, being full of the Holy Spirit, looked up steadfastly into heaven, and saw the glory of God, and Jesus standing on the right hand of God"—which shows that heaven is not so far away but that God can allow us to look into it, if He will. "And they stoned Stephen, calling upon God, and saying, Lord Jesus, receive my spirit." Thus we have it clearly established from Scripture teachings that not only is heaven the dwelling place of God the Father, but of Jesus Christ the Son. A great many think that there is but one person. There is but one God; but there are three persons, God the Father, God the Son, and God the Holy Spirit. When I get to heaven, I expect to see them all there. There is Christ standing on the right hand of God. Stephen saw Him. We have got Christ there; heaven would not be all that we love unless Christ was there. I would be unhappy, when I got to heaven, if I could not find Him there who redeemed me, who died for me, who bought me with His own blood. Someone asked a Christian man once what he expected to do when he got to heaven? He said he expected to spend the first thousand years in looking at Jesus Christ, and after that he would look for Peter, and then for James, and for John; and all the time he could conceive of would be joyfully filled with looking upon these great persons. But oh, it seems to me that one look at Jesus Christ will more than reward us for all that we have ever done for Him down here; for all the sacrifices we can possibly make for Him, just to see Him; and not only that, but we shall become like Him when we have seen Him, because we shall be like the Master Himself. Jesus, the Savior of the world, will be there. We shall see Him face to face.

It won't be the pearly gates, it won't be the jasper walls, and the streets paved with transparent gold, that shall make it heaven for us. These would not satisfy us. If these were all, we would not want to stay there forever. I heard the other day of a child whose mother was very sick; and while she lay very low, one of the neighbors took the child away to stay with her until the mother should be well again. But instead of getting better, the mother died; and they thought they would not take the child home until the funeral was all over; and would never tell her about her mother being dead. So awhile afterward they brought the little girl home. First she went into the sitting room to find her mother; then she went into the parlor, to find her mother there; and she went from one end of the house to the other and could not find her. At last she said, "Where is my mamma?" And when they told her her mamma was gone, the little thing wanted to go back to the neighbor's house again. Home had lost its attractions to her, since her mother was not there any longer. No; it is not the jasper walls and the pearly gates that are going to make heaven attractive. It is the being with God. We shall be in the presence of the Redeemer; we shall be forever with the Lord.

Angels Dwell in Heaven

We have now seen that God the Father and God the Son are dwelling in heaven. Will you turn to the eighteenth chapter of Matthew, verse 10: "Take heed that ye despise not one of these little ones; for I say unto you that in heaven their angels do always behold the face of my Father which is in heaven." So we shall have the company of angels when we go there. We find when Gabriel came down and told Zachariah that he should have a son, Zachariah doubted his word; and Gabriel replied: "I am Gabriel, that stands in the presence of God." It says in Luke 2:13 that after one angel had proclaimed that Jesus was born in Bethlehem, there was a multitude of the heavenly host telling out the wonderful story. So, we have angels in heaven. We have God the Father, and Christ the Son, and angels dwelling there. The angels, undoubtedly, wander away from the throne of God to this worldly sphere, to watch over the soul's welfare of those they have left behind. It may be that some angels are hovering over the souls here tonight, to see if someone will decide in favor of the Lord's side.

The Dead in Christ Dwell in Heaven

And we have not only the presence of the angels already established, but we have friends. Those who have died in the Lord are there. Do you believe that Stephen is not there, after his martyrdom? Do you believe God did not answer that prayer of his, "Lord, receive my spirit"? Undoubtedly, the moment that spirit left that body it winged its way to the world of light. Do you think those who have died in Christ are not there with the Master today? What does Paul mean when he says, "Absent from the body, present with the Lord"? All the redeemed ones are in heaven. We talk about "the best of earth." They are not down here. They are up in heaven. The best that ever trod this earth are up there, around the throne, singing their songs of praise, the sweetest song you ever heard. Turn to John 12:26: "If any man serve me, let him follow me; and where I am, there shall also my servant be; if any man serve me, him will my Father honor." I want to call your attention to this: "Where I am, there shall also my servant be." They shall be with Him. We have it clearly established. Will you turn to Revelation 7:9–10. "After this I beheld, and lo, a great multitude, which no man could number, of all nations, and kindreds, and people, and tongues, stood before the throne, and before the Lamb, clothed with white robes, and palms in their hands; and cried with a loud voice, saying, Salvation to our God which sitteth upon the throne, and unto the Lamb."

Is Your Name in the Book of Life?

There are redeemed saints around the throne. You may say: "Well, what good does that do me? That will not help me. What I want to know is, have I an interest in that land?" Well, I cannot speak for the rest of you; but I can say that it is the privilege of everyone in this audience to know that their names may be written in heaven, if they care to have them there. When the seventy went out to preach, in every town they went to there was a great revival. People are prejudiced against revivals in these days; but they are as old as the world. When these men went out, two by two, and proclaimed the gospel, their cry was, "Repent, for the kingdom of heaven is at hand"; and the seventy returned elated with their wonderful success. They thought all they had to do was to speak and the whole world would be moved. But they were told: "Rejoice not at your success in these cities; rejoice that your names are written in heaven." It is a grand thing for a man or woman to know that his or her name is written in heaven. Young woman, do you know today that your name is written there? Young man, do you know that your name is written in heaven? Do you think that Christ would have told these men to rejoice if He had not known that their names were written there? Some persons say that you cannot be sure; but that is one of the greatest delusions of the devil. If we cannot be certain of being saved, then we cannot preach salvation. There is not one passage of Scripture that gives us reason to doubt our own salvation. "I know that my Redeemer liveth"; in Him I believe. I know that I have passed in this world from death to life; I know, *I know*, I KNOW—that is the way the Scripture speaks in regard to our salvation. And so, if you do not know today that your name is written in heaven, if no spirit bears witness with your spirit that your name is written in heaven, oh, do not sleep tonight until you do know it! It is the privilege of every man and woman in this house to know it, if he or she will.

Turn back to the prophecy of Daniel a moment, chapter 12 and verse 1: "And at that time shall Michael stand up, the great prince which standeth for the children of thy people; and there shall be a time of trouble such as never was since there was a nation, even to that same time; and at that time thy people shall be delivered, every one that shall be found within the book." Every one that shall be found written—not in the church book; a good many have got their names written on some church record that have not got them written in the Book of Life; but every one whose name is found written in the Book of Life shall be delivered. Then would you turn a moment to Paul's epistle to the Philippians, fourth chapter, third verse: "And I entreat thee also, true yokefellow, help those women which labored with me in the gospel, with Clement, also, and with my other fellow-laborers whose names are in the Book of Life." Why, it is not only they themselves who know it, but Paul seemed to know their names are there. He sent them greeting, "whose names are in the Book of Life." My dear friend, is your name there? It seems to me it is a very sweet thought to think we can have our names there and know it; that we can send our names on ahead of us, and know they are written in the Book of Life.

I had a friend coming back from Europe, some time ago, and she came down with some other Americans from London to Liverpool. On the train down they were talking about the hotel they would stop at. They had to stay there

16 / Classic Sermons on Heaven and Hell

a day or two before the boat sailed; and so they all concluded to go to the Northwestern Hotel; but when they reached Liverpool, they found that the hotel was completely filled, and had been full for days. Every room was taken, and the party started to go out, but this lady did not go with them; and they asked her, "Why, are you not coming?" "No," said she; "I am going to stay here." "But how? The hotel is full." "Oh," said she, "I have got a room." "How did you get it?" "I telegraphed on a few days ago for one." Yes; she alone had taken pains to telegraph her name on ahead, and had thus secured her room. That is just what God wants you to do. Send your name on ahead. Have your mansion ready for you when you come to die. Don't go on neglecting this great question; don't neglect your soul's salvation; don't neglect your home beyond the grave.

You can have your name written in the Book of Life today, and have the crown and robe all ready for you when your spirit leaves your body. You can secure an interest in the kingdom of God this very day, if you will only seek it. But there is another passage I want to call your attention to in regard to this very point of having your names put in the Book of Life. Now turn to Revelation 13:8: "And all that dwell upon the earth shall worship him, whose names are not written in the Book of Life of the Lamb slain from the foundation of the world." Ah, there is a good deal in Scripture about our names being written in the Book of Life. Turn to Revelation 20:12: "And I saw the dead, small and great, stand before God; and the books were opened; and another book was opened which is the Book of Life; and the dead were judged out of those things which were written in the books, according to their works." Then in the last chapter but one, and the last verse: "And there shall in no wise enter into it anything that defileth, neither whatsoever worketh abomination, nor maketh a lie, but they which are written in the Lamb's Book of Life." Not a soul shall enter in through the pearly gates of that city whose names are not written in the Book of Life. It is a very important thing that we have our names written there; and then I think the next important thing after our names are written in the Book of Life is to have our children's there. We ought to be careful and see that the names of the children whom God has given us are written there.

Are Your Children's Names in the Book of Life?

I want to speak here for a few minutes about our children, for the promises are not only to us, but to our children. I pity those fathers and mothers who don't believe in the conversion of their little children. I pity the fathers and mothers who are not laboring to bring their children to Christ and have their names written in the Book of Life. I heard of a mother dying a few years ago of consumption; and when the hour came for her departure, she asked that her children be brought in, and the oldest child was brought to her bedside. The mother put her dying hand on his head, smoothed his hair, and gave him her dying blessing; and the next child was brought in, and the next, and the next, and to each she gave a message of love and hope. And at last the little infant was brought in; and she hugged it to her bosom and kissed it, and hugged it again and again until, as they went to take the little child from her mother, as they saw it was exciting her and hastening her death, she looked up into her husband's face and said: "I charge you to bring all these children home with you." And so God charges us parents to bring our children home with us. He doesn't want one left out, but wants every one written in the Book of Life. And they can be written there today if we only seek; and if that is uppermost in the minds of God's people, to have them there, they will be brought in. What a blessed revival we will have, if the fathers and mothers will only wake up and see that they are brought in! If we want to shine forever in the kingdom of God, then we must bring them in. But the trouble is, we want to shine down here in this fleeting world. How ambitious the fathers and the mothers are that their children shall just shine here for a little while; and the best and final interest of their soul is overlooked and forgotten.

I heard of a man that was dying some time ago, a man of great wealth; and when the doctor told him he could not live, the lawyer was sent for, to make out his will. And the dying man's little girl, only about four years old, did not understand what death meant; and when the mother told her that her papa was going away, the little child went to the bedside and looked into her father's eyes and asked, "Papa, have you got a home in that land that you are going to?" And the question sunk down deep into his soul. He had spent all his time and all his energy in the accumulation of great wealth. He had a grand home, and now had to leave it, and how that question came home to him.

Dear friends, let me ask you the question today: have you got a home beyond the grave? Can you say your name is written in the Lamb's Book of Life? Can you rejoice as only Christ's disciples rejoice, because your name is there? If you cannot, then don't let the sun go down until the great question of eternity is settled. Let the news flash over the wires of heaven, up to the throne of God, that you want your name there: "Oh, let my name be written in the Book of Life!" And then when your name is called, and there is a voice heard, "Come up hither!" you will go with joy and gladness to meet your Lord and Savior. You remember how it was with that dying soldier—you have undoubtedly seen it, it has been in print so often—who, lying on his cot, was heard to say, "Here! here! here!" and they went to him and asked him what he wanted. "Oh," said he, "they are calling the roll of heaven, and I am answering to my name"; and in a few minutes he faintly whispered it again, and was gone. That great roll is being called; and it will be a very important thing, more important than anything else when the hour comes, that our names be written in the Book of Life; for God says, except it is written in the Book of Life, we shall not enter that city. The gates will be closed against us; no one will enter the kingdom of God except those whose names are written in the Book of Life. So, my friends, let us be wise. Let us see that our names are there; and then let us go to work, and see if we cannot bring our children to Christ. I know a mother in this audience, today, who has got a family of children; a few days ago she got stirred up and thought she would go to her children and talk to them personally about Christ. She commenced only ten days ago, and what is the result? A son and two daughters—all that she has got—have been brought to Christ; and perhaps there is not a happier woman in New York today, because she has got the names of her family all written in the Book of Life. She knows that they are to be an unbroken circle in eternal life. Fathers and mothers, let us be wise unto eternity and bring our children into the kingdom with us. But you may say, What has this to do with heaven? You cannot talk about heaven, but the children must be spoke of, "For of such is the kingdom of heaven." They have been going up there for these six thousand years. Their little spirits are up yonder with the Shepherd; and He will take better care of them than we can. It seems as if it ought to make heaven very dear to us.

I never talk about children and heaven, but what the story of two fathers comes right home to me. One lived out in the western country, on the banks of the Mississippi river. The world calls him rich, but how poor he is, or, how poor he was! Thank God! he is rich now. One day his oldest son was brought home to him unconscious; a terrible accident had happened, and the family physician was hurriedly called in. As he came in, the father said: "Doctor, do you think my son will recover?" "No," said the doctor, "he is dying, and cannot recover." "Well," says the father, "only bring him to, can't you, that we may tell him? I don't want him to die without knowing that he is dying." The doctor said he would try, but that the boy was fast dying. After awhile the boy did become conscious for a moment, and the father cried: "My boy, the doctor tells me you are dying and cannot live. I could not let you die without letting you know it." The young man looked up to his father, and said: "Father, do you tell me I am going to die right away?" "Yes, my boy," said the agonized father; "you will be gone in a little while." "Oh, father, won't you pray for my lost soul?" Said the speechless father, "I cannot pray, my son." The boy grew unconscious, and after a little while was gone; and the father said when he buried that boy that if he could have called him back by prayer, he would have given all he was worth. He had been with that boy all those years, and had never prayed once for him. Am I talking to a prayerless father and mother today? Gather your children around you and show them the way to the kingdom of God. Train them to go where Christ reigns in triumph that they may be with you.

The other father was a contrast. I don't know but he may be in this audience this evening. His son had been dangerously ill, and when he came home one day he found his wife greatly troubled. She told him there had been a great change since morning, and she thought their boy was dying. "I wish," said she, "that you would go in and tell him of his condition, for I cannot bear to; and he ought to know it if he is dying." The father went in, went up to his son's bedside, placed his hand on the boy's pale forehead, and saw the cold, damp sweat of night was gathering, and he saw in a little while the boy would be gone; and he said, "My son, do you know you are dying?" And the young man said, "No; am I dying?" "Yes, my son." "Will I die today?" "Yes, my boy; you cannot live until night." And the boy looked surprised, and yet seemed to be glad, and said: "Well, father, I will be with Jesus, tonight, won't I?" "Yes, my boy; you will stand tonight with the Savior," and the father turned away to conceal his tears. And the boy saw the tears, and said: "Father, don't you weep for me; when I go to heaven, I will go right straight to Jesus and tell Him that ever since I can remember, you have tried to lead me to Him."

God has given me two little children; if I know my heart today, I would rather have such testimony as this go home to my Father, through my children, than to have the world rolled at my feet. I would rather have them come to my grave and drop a tear over it, and say: "When my father lived, he was more anxious for my eternal salvation than he was for my temporal good," than I would to have all the power this world can bestow. A few weeks ago, when my boy was sick, and I didn't know but that it would result fatally, I took my place by the side of his bed, and placed my hand on his forehead, and said: "Willie, suppose you should be really sick"—I didn't want to have him think he was likely to die—"and you should be taken away, do you think you would be afraid of death?" And a tear trickled down his cheek, as he said: "Last summer I was awful afraid of death; but Jesus has taken it all away now. If I die, I would go to Him; and He would give me everything I wanted." Ah! how sweet it was to think the little fellow was not afraid of death. It seems to me, we ought to teach our children so that they will hail with joy the time that they can go to meet Jesus, their blessed Savior. Oh, may the Spirit of the Lord God come upon this assembly tonight, and may we know that our names are written in the kingdom of heaven, and then see that the children whom God has given us are written in the Book of Life.

What Will the Faithful Do in Heaven?

Henry H. Savage (1887–1967) is best remembered for his thirty-eight years as pastor of the First Baptist Church, Pontiac, Michigan. One of the founders of the National Association of Evangelicals and of the Conservative Baptist Foreign Mission Society, Dr. Savage was active as an evangelist, missionary leader and conference speaker. While pastoring in Pontiac, he also directed the Maranatha Bible Conference in Muskegon, Michigan. A man burdened for world missions, he saw his two sons and his daughter go to the mission field to serve the Lord. Dr. Savage was the friend and mentor of many Christian leaders in Youth for Christ, Christian Businessmen's Committee, and various missionary organizations.

This message was given at the 1962 Moody Bible Institute Founder's Week Conference and was published in the book of 1962 conferences messages published by Moody Press. It is used by permission of Moody Press.

Henry H. Savage

2

WHAT WILL THE FAITHFUL DO IN HEAVEN?

He said therefore, A certain nobleman went into a far country to receive for himself a kingdom, and to return. And he called his ten servants, and delivered them ten pounds, and said unto them, Occupy till I come. But his citizens hated him, and sent a message after him, saying, We will not have this man to reign over us. And it came to pass, that when he was returned, having received the kingdom, then he commanded these servants to be called unto him, to whom he had given the money, that he might know how much every man had gained by trading. Then came the first, saying, Lord, thy pound hath gained ten pounds. And he said unto him, Well, thou good servant: because thou hast been faithful in a very little, have thou authority over ten cities. And the second came, saying, Lord, thy pound hath gained five pounds. And he said likewise to him, Be thou also over five cities (Luke 19:12–19).

VERY LITTLE IS said about the positive side of our future existence. We read books about heaven and we find there will be no pain, no sorrow, no grief, no parting, no sickness, no darkness, no nothing. But very little is said about what there *will* be in heaven. I want to think with you in terms of the positive side of some of the activities that we may be engaging in throughout eternity.

In Ephesians 1:3–5 we read: "Blessed be the God and Father of our Lord Jesus Christ, who hath blessed us with all spiritual blessings in heavenly places in Christ: according as he hath chosen us in him before the foundation of the world, that we should be holy and without blame before him in love: having predestinated us unto the adoption of children by Jesus Christ to himself, according to the good pleasure of his will."

Now I am going to ask you a question. Please do not

answer it yet; I am afraid you will answer it wrong. How many of you have been adopted into the family of God? I have not been, because, you see, I have been *born* into that family. There is a lot of difference between being adopted and being born into a family. *Adoption*, according to the dictionary, is the voluntary acceptance of a child of other parents to legally become the same as one's own child. But the nature of the child has not been changed. There is a change in the legal status but not in the parentage. He does not become a new creature.

In ancient Rome, a man could have a wife and several concubines. He could have children of both the wife and the concubines and they could be raised in the same home. But at the age of twenty-one, the child of the legal wife, the legitimate son, would be taken to the market and there "son-placed," or adopted. In that case, the word *adopted* would mean he would be placed in the position of assuming his share of the family responsibilities, engaging in the family business. (If you want to go into this a little further, you will find a note at the bottom of page 1250 of the *Scofield Bible*.)

This idea of having the son continue with the work of the father was found in ancient Israel. Usually the potter's son was a potter, a carpenter's son was a carpenter, a weaver's son was a weaver. Something of the same thing is found in the guilds of England: the son usually follows the business of the father. It is also true in the great casts of India. It is almost impossible for anyone to get out of one cast in India and become a member of another. Whatever the father's business is, becomes the son's business. Having been adopted, the son, according to the adoption principles of ancient Rome, would then be in the father's business, could sign legal papers and was legally heir of all his father's possessions.

We find then that God tells us we are to be adopted. But I will not be adopted until the time comes when God wants to put me in a place of eternal responsibility according to His will and His pleasure.

I have gone through all the books that I could locate on the subject of heaven and have read every article I could put my hands on, and I have found it almost impossible to find anything positive on our activities in heaven.

A couple of weeks ago I read through a recent digest of a much larger book on the general subject of eschatology—one that I think is about the best book there is on the subject—and the only conclusion I could come to from that book was that all the Lord or the saints will have to do throughout eternity is to judge this world and the people who are on the earth. I am certain the author does not believe that and he does not say it in so many words, but that is the implication.

But are the saints going to be limited to this earth? Let us look at a few verses. 1 Thessalonians 4:17: "We . . . shall be caught up together with them in the clouds, to meet the Lord in the air"—not to meet Him on the earth, but in the air—"so shall we ever be with the Lord." John 14:3–4: "And if I go and prepare a place for you"—not stay here to prepare a place, but go to prepare a place—"I will come again, and receive you unto myself; that where I am, there ye may be also."

Rulers of the New Creation

And what will the faithful be doing in heaven? Matthew 24:46–47: "Blessed is that servant, whom his lord when he cometh shall find so doing," that is, being faithful. "Verily I say unto you, that he shall make him ruler over all his goods." He is going to be a ruler. Matthew 25:19, 21, 23, where we have the story of the talents: "After a long time the lord of those servants cometh, and reckoneth with them . . . His lord said unto (one of them), Well done, thou good and faithful servant: thou hast been faithful over a few things, I will make thee ruler over many things: enter thou into the joy of thy lord . . . His lord said to (another), Well done, good and faithful servant; thou hast been faithful over a few things, I will make thee ruler over many things: enter thou into the joy of thy lord."

Now let us get back to the portion of God's Word in Luke that we read in the beginning. I believe that refers to the Lord Jesus Christ as the nobleman, having been rejected by the citizens of Israel and having gone to receive the kingdom, after which He will come back. In the meantime, the nobleman left a certain investment ($1,000) with each of his servants. This word *servants* is exactly the same word Paul uses concerning himself in Romans 1:1 where he speaks of being a servant or a bondslave of the Lord. The same word is found in Romans 6 where again it means a bondslave. Therefore it would seem that the word *servants* here refers to those of our Church Age to whom our Lord has given that which we might invest for Him. He said He would come back, and then He will call His servants before Him. One who is called before Him has gained $10,000 with the $1,000 given him. The Lord says, "All right, be over ten cities." Another one comes who has gained $5,000. He says, "All right, be over five cities. " Here was the fulfillment of the promise to those that were faithful—faithful enough to have gained even one thousand percent on the investment.

Suppose during this Christian era we have had one million faithful Christians who will be entitled to that sort of reward. Now, it says ten cities—not ten hamlets, or ten towns, or ten villages, or ten crossroads. If each one of this million is to have ten cities over which to rule, that means ten million cities. Where would you find room here on the earth for ten million cities? And another one will have five cities. Suppose there are two million people faithful enough to have five cities, that is ten million more cities. Where are you going to find them? There isn't room on this earth for all of them.

Let me tell you what I think. I believe the Lord Jesus Christ is going to spend eternity continually creating. In the process of that creation, there will be other planets to be populated and they will be given over to the charge of the faithful ones. Revelation 22:5 says: "And they shall reign forever and ever."

Partners with Christ

Recently I was reading Ephesians 2 in the Amplified Version of the New Testament. Here is verse 2: "And He raised us up together with Him and made us sit down together—giving us joint seating with Him—in the heavenly sphere."

We are to be united with Him, not here on earth but in the whole universe, the heavenly sphere; united with Him in ruling over the universe forever and forever, and helping Him to do whatever He has to do. For in Romans 8:16–17 we read: "The Spirit himself beareth witness with our spirit, that we are the children of God: and if children, then heirs; heirs of God, and joint-heirs with Christ."

Suppose when my father died he left an estate of $10,000, and suppose when the will was read we heard something like this: "I hereby bequeath my property of $10,000 to my two sons: to the elder son Hubbard (that's my brother), $9,999; to my younger son (that would be me), $1." We would both be heirs, but I would not be very happy over the situation. But suppose we opened the will and read something like this: "I hereby bequeath my property of $10,000 to my two sons as joint-heirs." What would that mean? That would mean that each one of us would receive $5,000.

God tells the faithful ones, "You are not only heirs with God, but joint-heirs with the Lord Jesus Christ, and whatever He is assigned to do throughout all eternity, you are to be partners with Him. "That is exactly what the word *adoption* means. We are to be adopted, not only into the family, but into the family's business. We are to be partakers with Him of the activities He is engaged in.

Dr. James M. Gray, who was president of Moody Bible Institute when I attended here back in 1911, wrote the book *Progress in the Life to Come*. Let me read a paragraph from that book:

> We know not what new worlds may be created, what new spheres may be opened for the exercise of the powers of those who shall reign in life . . . As the city descends out of heaven, may its dwellers never return thither again? The answer to this question is found in their relationship to an eternal union with Christ. Will He be restricted to a glory that is below the heavens? No, and no more will they who are associated with Him in His glory.

He who created the universe is certainly not going to be limited to this little speck we call earth. His activities will be throughout the whole universe—and we are to be associated with Him. Certain of the faithful will reign over this earth, since it is part of the universe, but they will not be left here exclusively as the activity in which they will be engaged.

Christ Creates All Things

What will the Lord Jesus Christ be doing throughout all eternity? In the first place, we know that He created all things. John 1:1–3: "In the beginning was the Word, the Word was with God, and the Word was God. The same was in the beginning with God. All things were made by him; and without him was not anything made that was made." And in verse 14 we find: "And the Word became flesh, and dwelt among us, (and we beheld his glory, the glory as of the only begotten of the Father)." The Son was the active agent of the Godhead in creating all things, and He is going to continue doing that. Williams' translation of Ephesians 4:10 says: "The very One that went down has gone up, too, far above all the heavens, to fill (or complete) the universe."

We'll think in a moment about the size of this universe, yet this universe does not fill all space by any means. Suppose we could take a trip to the very farthest galaxy. What would we see on the other side? More space. And when you got on the outer edge of all space and looked on the other side of that, what would you see? Just more space. It makes you dizzy to think about it, doesn't it? There is all that room for the Lord to keep on creating things throughout all the universe. That is what He says in Ephesians: He went down and has gone up far beyond the heavens, in order that He might continue to complete all things and to fill all things. And you and I are going to be joint-heirs with Him. We are going to be engaged in the work that He will be doing throughout all eternity—still creating, still fulfilling all the purposes of God Almighty.

Christ Holds All Things Together

In Colossians 1:16–17 we read of something else our Lord

is doing: "For by him were all things created, that are in heaven, and that are in earth, visible and invisible, whether they be thrones, or dominions, or principalities, or powers: all things were created by him, and for him: and he is before all things, and *by him all things consist.*" What does that word *consist* mean? To cohere, to be bound together.

When I went to school we learned that the atom was the very smallest possible division of matter; but within the past few years scientists have discovered that an atom is a universe in itself, filled with electrons, protons, neutrons and other subparticles, all held in relationship one to the other by electrical charges. It is this tremendous force within the atom which has been liberated to make the atomic bomb, and to release vast powers hitherto only dreamed of.

You ask a scientist what this power is. We can measure it, we can say it is there, we can deal with it, we can operate with it, but what is it? No scientist on the basis of mere science can tell us. But as Christians we know. Jesus Christ is the one who is atomic power; He is the one by whom all things consist. It is His power that holds all the various matters of the universe together. And I am going to be associated with Him, a joint-heir of His throughout all eternity, seated together with Him in the place of authority in handling the heavenly spheres!

Christ Upholds All Things

What else does the Lord Jesus Christ do? In Hebrews 1:3 we read of Him: "Who being the brightness of his glory, and the express image of his person, and upholding all things by the word of his power." Upholding all things, what does that mean? That means keeping things in their proper relationship to each other so that they do not fly apart. Why is it that in our solar system the planets keep going around at exactly an ascertained speed and we can tell exactly where a planet is going to be ten thousand years from now? What keeps these planets in their rotating spheres?

We call it gravitation. Not one of us is bound to the floor and yet the earth is traveling around at a tremendous speed. Why doesn't centrifugal force simply throw everything off the surface of the earth? Because of the power of gravitation. Isaac Newton was sitting under an apple tree one time when an apple fell off and hit him on the head and he discovered gravitation.

We can measure gravitation. When you step on the scales you are measuring gravitation. We can deal with gravitation; we can deal with its laws. But what is gravitation? On the basis of pure science, no scientist can tell us. But you and I know because God tells us. He is the One who is the upholder of all things. My Lord's power is displayed in the power of gravitation.

You say, "Mr. Savage, you are crazy!" Well, at least I have an answer, which is more than anyone who denies the Lord has, and the answer is based on God's Word. And I'm going to be associated with Him in running the affairs of the universe throughout all eternity.

The Lord's universal and unqualified rule will be from heaven. I have been suggesting that right along, but let us look into it a little further. Going back to Ephesians 4:10, now reading from the Authorized Version: "He that descended is the same also that ascended up far above *all* heavens." What do we mean by heavens? There are three heavens mentioned in the Bible. There is the atmospheric heaven, the starry heaven, and the heaven which is beyond the starry heaven. The record tells us Christ has ascended beyond all heavens. How far is that? Astronomers tell us they have discovered light from stars that they compute to be at least five hundred million light years away. So that particular star from which the light is coming must have been created at least five hundred million years ago. Suppose that star had stopped shining five hundred million years ago. We would not know it until now, with light traveling 186,000 miles a second. If you could light a candle and somehow project that light around the world, it would go around seven times before you could blow it out; in one second's time, seven times around the earth. And yet here is a star five hundred million light years away.

Now, if Jesus at His ascension went far beyond all the heavens and He traveled at the rate of light, He would not be there yet, He would not be there for almost five hundred million years, and He couldn't possibly come back for another five hundred million years. So I guess we don't need to look forward to the Rapture for some time, do we? Would you say that it would take the Lord that long?

You may disagree with me on some of my interpretations of the Bible, but I believe that when Jesus told Mary, "Don't touch me, for I haven't yet been to my Father and reported," He was the High Priest who had to report that the sacrifice was complete and the penalty had been paid for the sins of the people; everything had been taken care of satisfactorily. Later He said, "Handle me and see, for a spirit hath not flesh and bones as ye see me have." What had happened in the meantime? Jesus, I believe, had presented Himself before the Father and said, "The work of atonement has been done," and then He came back again. How long did it take Him to do it? He went more than five hundred million light years away, but He was away only a very few hours at the most!

That is not the most incredible thing. In Acts 14 we find that Paul was stoned and left for dead, but suddenly he got up and walked back into town. Later he referred to this incident in 2 Corinthians 12:2–4. "I knew a man in Christ above fourteen years ago, (whether in the body, I cannot tell; or whether out of the body, I cannot tell: God knoweth;) such an one caught up to the third heaven. And I knew such a man, (whether in the body, or out of the body, I cannot tell: God knoweth;) how that he was caught up into paradise, and heard unspeakable words, which it is not lawful for a man to utter." That is, he heard things he couldn't repeat because there were no words in the language by which he could translate them, they were so marvelous, so wonderful, so far beyond any comparison you might make.

Where had he gone? He said he went to the third heaven—beyond the starry heaven, more than five hundred million light years away, and he had been up there and back in just a little while. How fast did he go? Well, he went farther than jets, and he went faster than jets. Do you know how fast I think he went? He went as fast as thought.

You say, "Mr. Savage, you are crazy!" It's wonderful to be crazy along this line of trying to think in terms of what heaven must be, the glories of it, the activities of it, the expanse of it. And you and I are joint-heirs with the Lord Jesus Christ, in control of the whole universe together with Him, ruling and reigning with Him.

Some weeks ago I spoke before a group of Pontiac businessmen, bankers, leading city officials and several school officials. I said, "You know, I've been here in Pontiac for thirty-eight years and there have been two things I have beet trying to do. In the first place, I have been trying to give away shares in the kingdom of heaven. I have been trying to give folks the right to say 'I am a shareholder.' As a child of God and a joint-heir with Jesus Christ, I am a shareholder. And I've been trying to give away shares."

Isn't it strange that some people put forth every effort to get away from the mercy of God. You don't blame those who are trying to hide from police officials if they have committed a crime, but why do you have to plead with people, Won't you get right with God that you may be a shareholder in the kingdom of God?

"But I have been going further than that. Not only have I been trying to give away shares in the kingdom, but I have been trying to sell stock. Now, what is the difference between a shareholder and a stockholder? As a stockholder one receives returns from the stock. Since I'm an heir of His, I am going to be able to reap the rewards of my faithfulness throughout all eternity, and the more stock I am willing to invest in, the more returns I will receive through all eternity."

Matthew 5:11–12: "Blessed are ye, when men shall revile you, and persecute you, and shall say all manner of evil against you falsely, for my sake. Rejoice, and be exceeding glad: for great is your reward in heaven." The next time somebody says mean things about you, just say, "Thank you, I am certainly glad to be talked about that way, because that means I'm going to have a little more reward in heaven." But, you know, we usually complain when we are not treated just the way we think we should be, and we get our feelings hurt. What a mess we make of things. Yet our Lord says, Blessed are ye . . . happy are ye . . . rejoice. Great is your reward, not here upon earth, but in heaven.

Matthew 6:19-20: "Lay not up for yourselves treasures upon earth, where moth and rust doth corrupt, and where thieves break through and steal: but lay up for yourselves treasures in heaven, where neither moth nor rust doth corrupt, and where thieves do not break through nor steal." Matthew 19:21: "If thou wilt be perfect, go and sell that thou hast, and give to the poor, and thou shalt have treasure in heaven."

All these verses look forward to the heavenly occupation, as I am adopted into the family of God to share His responsibilities and His work.

Who Will Rule with Him?

But, you know, God isn't going to take just anybody who comes along. He isn't going to say, "Well, as long as you have accepted my Son, that's all there is to it." No, there is more to it than that. God can share these eternal responsibilities only with those whom He can trust, with those whom He has tried and proved, with those who have been able to pass the examination. God has certain requirements, certain standards for those who are to be associated with His Son in ruling the affairs of the universe forever and ever. We must meet these standards if we are going to be found among those whom He can consider worthy of receiving such an exalted position in heaven. This we must do if we are interested in having the opportunity of saying, "I would like to have a great reward."

Well, is that a good incentive for a Christian? Of course it is, otherwise He would not always be urging us to do the things which provide for a reward. Since He is constantly urging us to do it, then let us say, "God, I do want to have an exalted position in heaven. I do want to be able not only to take my place with the Lord Jesus Christ in running the affairs of the universe, but to be united with Him as He continues creating and reaching out through space with more universes. I want to be associated with Him."

You know, I'm not a bit sorry I'm a Christian. How could anybody, at any time, think in terms of Christianity being anything but the most marvelous investment that you and I can make?

Heaven

John Charles Ryle (1816–1900) was an evangelical leader in the Anglican Church in Great Britain, serving several churches and then serving as dean of Norwich. He was named the first bishop of Liverpool. Conservative in theology, he wrote over one hundred popular tracts and booklets as well as books of Christian biography and biblical studies, his *Expository Thoughts on the Gospels* being perhaps his most famous. A defender of the "old Reformation faith," Ryle was criticized by some evangelicals for not leaving the Anglican Church, but he felt God called him to bear witness to the truth in the church where God placed him.

This sermon was originally published in 1900 in his book *The Christian Race*, which was reprinted by Baker Book House in 1978 as *The True Christian*.

John Charles Ryle

3
HEAVEN

There shall in no wise enter into it any thing that defileth, neither whatsoever worketh abomination, or maketh a lie: but they which are written in the Lamb's Book of Life (Revelation 21:27).

BRETHREN THERE CAN be no question about the place described in our text: it is heaven itself, that holy city, the new Jerusalem, which is yet to be revealed.

I would gladly begin this my last Sunday among you by speaking of heaven. Before I depart and leave you in the wilderness of this world, I would dwell a little on that Canaan God has promised to them that love Him; *there* it is the last and best wish of my heart you may all go; *there* it is my consolation to believe I shall at all events meet some of you again.

Brethren, you all hope to go to heaven yourselves. There is not one of you but wishes to be in happiness after death. But on what are your hopes founded? Heaven is a prepared place; they that shall dwell there are all of one character, the entrance into it is only by one door. Brethren, remember that. And then, too, I read of two sorts of hope: a good hope and a bad hope; a true hope and a false hope; a lively hope and a dead hope; the hope of the righteous and the hope of the wicked, of the believer and of the hypocrite. I read of some who have hope through grace, a hope that maketh not ashamed, and of others who have no hope and are without God in the world. Brethren, remember that. Surely it were wise and prudent and safe to find out what the Bible tells you on the subject, to discover whether your confidence is indeed well founded, and to this end I call your attention to the doctrine of my text. There you will find three things:

1. There is mention of the place itself.
2. We are told the character of those who will certainly not be there, and
3. Who alone will be there.

The Lord grant you may consider well your own fitness for heaven. There must be a certain meetness for that blessed place in our minds and characters. It is senseless, vain, and absurd to suppose that all shall go there, whatever their lives have been. May God the Holy Spirit incline you to examine yourselves faithfully while you have time, before that great day comes when the unconverted shall be past all hope and the saints past all fear.

1. There Is Mention of the Place Itself

There is such a place as heaven. No truth is more certain in the whole of Scripture than this, there remains a rest for the people of God. This earth is not our rest; it cannot be; there breathes not man or woman who ever found it so. Go, build your happiness on earth, if you are so disposed; choose everything you can fancy would make life enjoyable—take money, house, and lands; take learning, health, and beauty; take honor, rank, obedience, troops of friends; take everything your mind can picture to itself or your eye desire—take all, and yet I dare to tell you even then you would not find rest. I know well that a few short years, and your heart's confession would be, it is all hollow, empty, and unsatisfying; it is all weariness and disappointment; it is all vanity and vexation of spirit. I know well you would feel within a hungering and famine, a leanness and barrenness of soul; and ready indeed would you be to bear your testimony to the mighty truth, "This earth is not our rest."

O brethren, how faithful is that saying, "If in this life only we have hope, we are indeed most miserable." This life, so full of trouble and sorrow and care, of anxiety and labor and toil; this life of losses and bereavements, of partings and separations, of mourning and woe, of sickness and pain; this life of which even Elijah got so tired that he requested he might die; truly I would be crushed to the very earth with misery, if I felt this life were all. If I thought there was nothing for me beyond the dark, cold, silent, lonely grave, I should indeed say, "Better never have been born." Thanks be to God this life is not all. I know and am persuaded there is a glorious rest beyond the tomb; this earth is only the training school for eternity, these graves are but the steppingstone and halfway house to heaven. I feel assured this my poor body shall rise again; this corruptible shall yet put on incorruption, and this mortal immortality, and be with Christ forever. Yes, heaven is truth and no lie. I will not doubt it. I am not more certain of my own existence than I am of this, there does remain a rest for the people of God.

What sort of a place shall heaven be? Before we pass on and consider its inhabitants, let us just pause an instant and think on this. What sort of a place shall heaven be? Heaven shall be a place of perfect rest and peace. They that dwell *there* have no more conflict with the world, the flesh, and the devil; their warfare is accomplished, and their fight is fought; at length they may lay aside the armor of God, at last they may say to the sword of the Spirit, "Rest and be still." They watch no longer, for they have no spiritual enemies to fear; they fast and mortify the flesh no longer, for they have no vile earthy body to keep under; they pray no more, for they have no evil to pray against. *There* the wicked must cease from troubling; *there* sin and temptation are forever shut out; the gates are better barred than those of Eden, and the devil shall enter in no more. O Christian brethren, rouse and take comfort; surely this shall be indeed a blessed rest. *There* shall be no need of means of grace, for we shall have the end to which they are meant to lead; *there* shall be no need of sacraments, we shall have the substance they are appointed to keep in mind; *there* faith shall be swallowed up in sight, and hope in certainty, and prayer in praise, and sorrow in joy. Now is the school time, the season of the lesson and the rod, then will be the eternal holiday. Now we must endure hardness and press on faint yet pursuing, then we shall sit down at ease, for the Canaanite shall be expelled forever from the land. Now

38 / Classic Sermons on Heaven and Hell

we are tossed upon a stormy sea, then we shall be safe in harbor. Now we have to plow and sow, there we shall reap the harvest; now we have the labor, but then the wages; now we have the battle, but then the victory and reward. Now we must bear the cross, but then we shall receive the crown. Now we are journeying through the wilderness, but then we shall be at home. O Christian brethren, well may the Bible tell you, "Blessed are the dead that die in the Lord, for they rest from their labor." Surely you must feel that witness is true.

But again. Heaven shall be a place of perfect and unbroken happiness. Mark what your Bible tells you in the very chapter which contains my text, "God shall wipe away all tears from the eyes of His people; and there shall be no more death, neither sorrow, nor crying, neither shall there be any more pain: for the former things are passed away." Hear what the prophet Isaiah says in the twenty-fifth chapter: "The Lord God will wipe away tears from off all faces; and the rebuke of His people shall He take away from off all the earth. And it shall be said in that day, Lo, this is our God; we have waited for Him and He will save us: this is the Lord; we have waited for Him, we will be glad and rejoice in His salvation." Brethren, think of an eternal habitation in which there is no sorrow. Who is there here below that is not acquainted with sorrow? It came in with thorns and thistles at Adam's fall, it is the bitter cup that all must drink, it is before us and behind us, it is on the right hand and the left, it is mingled with the very air we breathe. Our bodies are racked with pain, and we have sorrow; our worldly goods are taken from us, and we have sorrow; we are encompassed with difficulties and troubles, and we have sorrow; our friends forsake us and look coldly on us, and we have sorrow; we are separated from those we love, and we have sorrow; those on whom our hearts' affections are set go down to the grave and leave us alone, and we have sorrow. And then, too, we find our own hearts frail and full of corruption, and that brings sorrow. We are persecuted and opposed for the gospel's sake, and that brings sorrow; we see those who are near and dear to us refusing to walk with God, and that brings sorrow. Oh, what a sorrowing, grieving world we live in!

Blessed be God! there shall be no sorrow in heaven. There shall not be one single tear shed within the courts above. There shall be no more disease and weakness and decay; the coffin, and the funeral, and the grave, and the dark-black mourning shall be things unknown. Our faces shall no more be pale and sad; no more shall we go out from the company of those we love and be parted asunder—that word, *farewell*, shall never be heard again. There shall be no anxious thought about tomorrow to mar and spoil our enjoyment, no sharp and cutting words to wound our souls; our wants will have come to a perpetual end, and all around us shall be harmony and love. O Christian brethren, what is our light affliction when compared to such an eternity as this? Shame on us if we murmur and complain and turn back, with such a heaven before our eyes! What can this vain and passing world give us better than this? This is the city of our God Himself, when He will dwell among us Himself. The glory of God shall lighten it, and the Lamb is the light thereof. Truly we may say, as Mephibosheth did to David, "Let the world take all, forasmuch as our Lord will come in peace." Such is the Bible heaven, there is none other; these sayings are faithful and true, not any of them shall fail. Surely, brethren it is worth a little pain, a little laboring, a little toil, if only we may have the lowest place in the kingdom of God.

2. Who Shall *Not* Enter Heaven?

Let us now pass on and see that great thing which is revealed in the second part of our text. You have heard of heaven; but all shall not enter it: and who are the persons who shall not enter in?

Brethren, this is a sad and painful inquiry, and yet it is one that must be made. I can do no more than declare to you Scripture truth; it is not my fault if it is cutting and gives offense. I must deliver my Master's message and diminish nothing; the line I have to draw is not mine, but God's: the blame, if you will lay it, falls on the Bible not on me. "There shall in no wise enter into heaven any thing that defileth, neither whatsoever worketh abomination, or maketh a lie." Verily these are solemn words; they ought to make you think.

"*Nothing that defileth.*" This touches the case of all who are defiled with sins of heart, and yet feel it not, and refuse to be made clean. These may be decent persons outwardly, but they are vile and polluted within. These are the worldly-minded. They live to this world only, and they have no thought of anything beyond it. The care of this world, the money, the politics of this world, the business of this world, the pleasures of this world, these things swallow up their whole attention and as for St. James' advice to keep ourselves unspotted from the world, they know not what it means.

These are the men who set their affections on earthly things; they have each their idol in the chamber of their imagination, and they worship and serve it more than God. These are the proud and self-righteous, the self-honoring and the self-conceited; they love the praise of men, they like the good opinion of this world, and as for the glorious Lord who made them, His honor, His glory, His house, His word, His service—these are all things which in their judgment must go down, and take the second place. These people know not what sorrow for sin means. They are strangers to spiritual anxiety; they are self-satisfied and content with their condition, and if you attempt to stir them up to zeal and repentance it is more than probable they are offended. Brethren, you know well there are such people; they are not uncommon; they may be honorable in the eyes of men, they may be wise and knowing in this generation, admirable men of business, they may be first and foremost in their respective callings, but still there is but one account of them; they bring no glory to their Maker, they are lovers of themselves more than of God, and therefore they are counted as defiled in His sight and nothing that is defiled shall enter heaven.

"*Nothing that worketh abomination.*" This touches the case of all who practice those sins of life which God has pronounced abominable, and take pleasure in them, and countenance those who practice them. These are the men who work the works of the flesh, each as his heart inclines him. These are the adulterers, fornicators, and unclean livers; these are the drunkards, revelers, and gluttons; these are the blasphemers, swearers, and liars. These are the men who count it no shame to live in hatred, variance, wrath, strife, envyings, quarrellings and the like. They throw the reins on the neck of their lusts; they follow their passions wherever they may lead them; their only object is to please themselves.

Brethren, you know well there are such people. The world may give smooth names to their conduct, the world may talk of them as light and happy, and loose and wild, but it will not do. They are all abominable in the sight of God, and except they be converted and born again, they shall in no wise enter heaven.

"Nothing that maketh a lie." This touches the case of hypocrites. These are the false professors; the lip-servants; they say that they know God, but in works they deny Him; they are like barren fig trees, all leaves and no fruit; they are like tinkling cymbals, all sound, but hollow, empty and without substance; these have a name to live while they are dead, and a form of godliness without the power. They profess what they do not practice, they speak what they do not think, they say much and do little, their words are most amazing, their actions are most poor. These men can talk most bravely of themselves; no better Christians than they are, if you will take them at their own valuation. They can talk to you of grace, and yet they show none of it in their lives; they can talk to you of saving faith, and yet they possess not that charity which is faith's companion. They can declaim against forms most strongly, and yet their own Christianity is a form and no more; they can cry out loudly against Pharisees, and yet there are no greater Pharisees than they are themselves.

Oh, no; this religion is of a sort that is public, and not private; plenty abroad, but none at home; plenty without, but none within; plenty in the tongue, but none in the heart. They are altogether unprofitable, good for nothing, they bear no fruit.

Brethren, you must know well there are such miserable persons; alas! the world is full of them in these latter days. They may deceive ministers, they may deceive their neighbors, they may even deceive their friends and families, they may try hard to deceive themselves; but they are no better than liars in God's sight, and except they repent, they shall in no wise enter heaven.

Brethren, consider well these things: "the sin-defiled, the abominable, the hypocrite, shall in no wise enter into heaven." Look well to your own souls; judge yourselves that you be not judged of the Lord; I call heaven and earth to witness this day, they that will live these bad lives, whether they be churchmen or dissenters, old or young, rich or poor, *they shall* in no wise enter in. Go, cleave to the ways of the world if you are so determined, stick to your sins if you must keep them, but I warn you solemnly this hour, they that will have these things shall in no wise enter in. Go, blame me now for speaking sharply to you—think I am too particular if you like it—but, oh! remember if you ever stand without the gates, crying, "Lord, open to us," in vain, remember there was a time when I told you, the worldly-minded and the evil livers shall in no wise enter in. Brethren, I have told you before, and I tell you now again for the last time, if you will cling to the things that God hates, you shall in no wise enter into heaven.

3. Who *Shall* Enter Heaven?

Brethren, we must pass on. The text has told you who shall not enter heaven. Oh! what a mighty crowd those words shut out! But it tells you something more: who are they that shall enter. Short is the account and simple: "They only that are written in the Lamb's Book of Life." What is this Book of Life? There is a book, a little book, a book prepared from all eternity, which God the Father keeps sealed—the book of His election; of that book man knows nothing, excepting this blessed truth that there is such a book. With that book man has little or nothing to do. But there is another book, a little book, a book belonging specially to the Lord Jesus Christ, a book still unfinished, though year after year there are more names written in it; a book still open, still ready to receive the names of believing penitents: there are still some blank pages left for you; and this is the Lamb's Book of Life. And who are written in this precious book? I do not know their names, but I do know their characters, and what those characters are I will endeavor to tell you shortly, for the last time.

They are all true penitents. They have been convinced of their own unworthiness in God's sight; they have felt themselves to be sinners in deed and in truth; they have mourned over their sins, hated their sins, forsaken their sins; the remembrance of their sins is grievous, the burden of them intolerable; they have ceased to think well of their own condition and count themselves fit to be saved; they have confessed with their whole heart: "Lord, we are really chief of sinners—Lord, we are indeed unclean."

They are all believers in Christ Jesus. They have found out the excellency of the work He did to save them, and cast on Him the burden of their souls. They have taken Christ for their all in all: their wisdom, their righteousness, their justification, their forgiveness, their redemption. Other payment of their spiritual debts they have seen none; other deliverances from the devil they have not been able to find. But they have believed on Christ, and come to Christ for salvation; they are confident that what they cannot do Christ can do for them, and having Jesus Christ to lean on, they feel perfect peace.

They are all born of the Spirit and sanctified. They have all put off the old man with his deeds, and put on the new man which is after God. They have all been renewed in the spirit of their minds; a new heart and a new nature has been given to them. They have brought forth those fruits which only are the proof of the Spirit being in them. They may have slipped and come short in many things; they may have mourned over their own deficiencies full often; but still, the general bent and bias of their lives has always been toward holiness—more holiness, more holiness, has always been their hearts' desire. They love God, and they must live to Him. Such is the character of them that are written in heaven. These, then, are the men whose names are to be found in the Lamb's Book of Life.

Once they may have been as bad as the very worst—defiled, abominable, liars: what matter? they have repented and believed, and now they are written in the Book of Life. They may have been despised and rejected of this world, poor and mean and lowly in the judgment of their neighbors: what matter? They had repentance and faith and new hearts, and now they are written in the glorious Book of Life. They may have been of different ranks and nations; they may have lived at different ages, and never seen each other's faces: what matter? They have one thing at least in common, they have repented and believed, and have been born again, and therefore they stand all together in the Lamb's Book of Life.

Yes, brethren, these are the men and women that enter heaven; nothing can keep them out. Tell me not of deathbed evidences, and visions and dreams of dying people; there is no evidence like that of Christ's followers—repentance, faith, and holiness; this is a character against which the gates shall never be closed. Repent and believe in Christ and be converted, and then, whatever happens to others, you, at least, shall enter heaven; you shall in no wise be cast out.

Certain of Heaven

And now, men and brethren, in conclusion, let me press upon you my old question. How is it with you? What, no answer! Are you ready to depart? Again, no answer! Is your name written in the Book of Life? Once more, have you no answer?

Oh, think, think, unhappy man or woman, whoever you are, think what a miserable thing it is to be uncertain about eternity. And then consider, if you cannot give your heart to God now, how is it possible you could enjoy God's heaven hereafter. Heaven is unceasing godliness; it is to be in the presence of God and His Christ forevermore. God is the light, the food, the air of heaven. It is an eternal Sabbath. To serve God is heaven's employment, to talk with God is heaven's occupation.

O sinners, sinners, could you be happy there? To which of all the saints would you join yourselves, by whose side would you go and sit down, with whom of all the prophets and apostles would you love to converse? Surely it would be a wearisome thing to you; surely you would soon want to go forth and join your friends outside. Oh, turn, turn while it is called today! God will not alter heaven merely to please you; better a thousand times to conform to His ways while you can. You must love the things of heaven before your death, or else you cannot enter heaven when you die.

Christian, look up and take comfort. Jesus has prepared a place for you, and they that follow Him shall never perish, neither shall any man pluck them out of His hands. Look forward to that glorious abode He has provided; look forward in faith, for it is yours. O Christian brethren, think what a glorious meeting that shall be. There we shall see the saints of old, of whom we have so often read; there we shall see those holy ministers whose faith and patience we have admired; there we shall see one another around the throne of our common Savior, and be parted and separated no more. There we shall labor and toil no more, for the days of mourning shall be ended. Oh, but my heart will leap within me, if I see there faces I have known among you; if I hear the names of any of you! The Lord grant it, the Lord bring it to pass. The Lord grant we may some of us, at least, come together in that day, when there shall be one fold and one Shepherd, and with one heart and voice join that glorious song, "Worthy is the Lamb that was slain; blessing and honor and glory and power be unto the Lamb forever and ever."

The Homesickness of the Soul

William E. Sangster (1900–1960) was the "John Wesley" of his generation as he devoted his life to evangelism and the promotion of practical sanctification. He pastored in England and Wales, and his preaching ability attracted the attention of the Methodist leaders. He ministered during World War II at Westminster Central Hall, London, where he pastored the church, managed an air-raid shelter in the basement, and studied for his Ph.D. at the London University. He served as president of the Methodist Conference (1950) and director of the denomination's home missions and evangelism ministry. He published several books on preaching, sanctification, and evangelism, as well as volumes of sermons.

This message comes from *Westminster Sermons*, Volume 1, published in 1960 by The Epworth Press, London.

William E. Sangster

4

THE HOMESICKNESS OF THE SOUL

At home with the Lord (2 Corinthians 5:8, RV).

ALL STUDENTS OF natural history know of the wonderful instinct of direction displayed by birds, and beasts, and fish. It is sometimes called "the homing instinct."

Cats and dogs often find their way back across wide stretches of unknown country. Pigeons fly direct to their homes hundreds of miles away. Seabirds carried around the coast from one side of England to the other return unerringly (apparently straight over the land) to the very cliff or burrow from which they were removed. Swallows, and other migrant birds, take a confident aerial journey between destinations thousands of miles apart. Salmon return to spawn in the rivers of their birth. Young eels steer their way through a wide heaving ocean to hereditary waters which they have never seen. Nothing in all nature is more wonderful than this amazing instinct of the lower creation for home.

The question has sometimes been raised whether or not man ever possessed this same homing instinct and lost it through the ages in his preoccupation with other things. The query is usually waived aside either with a direct negative or by the assertion that the evidence is too slight for an answer to be given.

I want to raise the question again. There is a deeper answer to it than most inquirers have guessed; a *spiritual* answer. Deep in the heart of man there is a homing instinct, profound, persistent, ineradicable, which he often ignores and might even deny, but which, if he turned his attention to it, might make him realize the inwardness of a line in the hymnbook at which, in other moods, he would be openly amused: "Heaven is my home."

I am aware, as I begin, that some among you will deny the very idea of it, but I base my argument on two undeniable facts of human nature, and, if you resist my inference at the end, you have still to explain those facts in some other way.

There Is Something in Man Which Earth Can Never Satisfy

I want to lay it down, first, as quite incontrovertible that *there is something in man which earth can never satisfy*. It is common for people to say and to believe that if they only had this or that coveted thing they would always be happy, and some of them die believing it. But the evidence of those who obtain the "treasure" does not bear them out. It satisfied for a little while . . . and then there was the old, persistent hunger again, clamorous as ever.

No one will deny that to lack enough *money* to meet the simple needs of life is to miss happiness, but it is a widespread error to suppose that a lot of money means a lot of joy. Jay Gould, the famous American millionaire, who died possessing fifty million dollars, summed up his life (not in a mood of despondency, but as his wrought-out and considered verdict on himself) in these words: "I suppose I am the most miserable devil on earth."

Some people set their mind on a coveted *position* and believe that complete satisfaction for them would come by its achievement; they work and scheme and plan to obtain that high post, but the satisfaction of arriving soon fades. When Benjamin Disraeli, twice Prime Minister of England, reviewed his life, he said: "Youth is a mistake; manhood a struggle; old age a regret." He may have been posing again, but men who could never be accused as *poseurs* have echoed his words.

Fame is the will-o'-the-wisp which beckons others on. Milton, you will remember, called fame "that last infirmity of noble mind." Sir Walter Scott achieved it—great, and worthy, and deserved fame—but there was that in him which not all the praise of men could satisfy. When he was dying he said, "Bring me the book."

"The book?" they said. "What book?"

"There is only *one* book," he answered a little wearily. "Bring me the Bible."

Pleasure is the goal of other people. Its pursuit becomes a science with them. The art of life, as they conceive it, is to squeeze from every moment the utmost pleasure it will yield, but so often it turns to gall and bitterness at the last. Byron may be taken as typical of the grosser hedonists. He drifted, in the quest of pleasure, from one woman to another, and died an old man at thirty-six, saying of himself on his last birthday:

> My days are in the yellow leaf;
> The flowers and fruits of love are gone;
> The worm, the canker, and the grief
> Are mine alone!

Some people pursue *physical health*; indeed, cults have grown up which make the fitness of this human form the end of all striving; but there are spiritual maladies which no harmony of the body can really cure and which, if uncured, will rob the body of its health as well.

I lived in a town once where lived also a doctor who had forsaken normal medical practice in order to advise people on how not to be ill and who was himself such a picture of physical fitness that people came from miles around to consult him about health. But I remember also the morning he came early to my door in agony of heart to tell of a deep malady in his own soiled soul and to ask my advice upon a moral problem which was grave indeed.

Now, that is my first point. There is something in man which earth cannot satisfy; not even the best things of earth. The testimony of those who have achieved coveted things is emphatic and uniform; there still remains a longing, and a hunger, and a heartache which nothing material or terrestrial seems able to meet. We live on earth and yet, somehow, we do not *belong* to it. In certain ways we have kinship with the beasts but, so far as we can judge, earth satisfies them.

> Irks care the crop-full bird?
> Frets doubt the maw-crammed beast?

Earth does not satisfy us. I cannot help but feel that that is an impressive fact. I warn you against supposing that, if only you had more of this or more of that, you would be completely satisfied. It is an illusion. Earth *cannot* satisfy you. William Watson—in his poem "World Strangeness"—asked:

> In this house with starry dome,
> Floored with gemlike plains and seas,
> Shall I never feel at home,
> Never wholly be at ease?

Never!
You weren't meant to.

There Is in Man a Nostalgia for Heaven

Here is the second fact. I believe that *there is in man a nostalgia for heaven.* Forgive me for reminding you that the word *nostalgia* comes from two Greek words: *nostos* meaning "return home"; and *alos*, meaning "pain." It meant originally homesickness as an incurable malady; incurable by anything—except, of course, by *home.*

Now, I believe that although it is hidden, ignored, overlaid, and even denied, there is in man a homesickness for heaven. Wordsworth, in his famous ode on "Intimations of Immortality from Recollections of Early Childhood," speaks with plainness of this secret reminiscence in the soul. He says:

> Our birth is but a sleep and a forgetting:
> The Soul that rises with us, our life's Star,
> Hath had elsewhere its setting,
> And cometh from afar:
> Not in entire forgetfulness,
> And not in utter nakedness,
> But trailing cloud of glory do we come
> From God, who is our home.

"From God, *who is our home!*"

All that Wordsworth had in mind when he said that is beyond the range of our present interest, but I *do* believe that there is in man a homesickness for heaven; that that ache which earth cannot satisfy can be satisfied by God; that all feel it, but only some understand it; that in a deeper sense than Cleopatra meant we might each truly say: "I have immortal longings in me."

There is an old legend of the Western Isles concerning a sea king who desired the company of a human being. One day he heard in his cavern under the sea a cry—a little human cry—and rose to the surface of the water to discover a child in a derelict boat. Just as he was about to make for the little vessel and take the child, a rescue party intervened, and he missed his prize. But—so the legend says—as they drew away with the one so nearly lost, the sea king cupped his hand and threw into the heart of the child a little sea-salt wave, and said as he submerged: "The child is mine. When it grows, the salt sea will call him and he will come home to me at the last."

It is only a Gaelic legend, but it enshrines the timeless truth. God has put in the heart of everyone of us a longing for Himself. The mass of men do not understand it. They just know that there are times when they want to be quiet; times when they want to be alone; times when the calendar, or the stars, or death speaks to them. They *hunger* and they *thirst* . . . but for what?

It is part of the service of religion to make the hunger of our souls clear to us; and that is why this nostalgia is known in its true meaning only among the devout. Our fathers sang:

> Strangers and pilgrims here below,
> This earth, we know, is not our place;
> But hasten through the vale of woe,
> And, restless to behold Thy face,
> Swift to our heavenly country move,
> Our everlasting home above.

And, as the song swelled and the certainty of self-understanding gripped their hearts, they burst into this glorious verse:

> Through Thee, who all our sins hast borne,
> Freely and graciously forgiven,
> With songs to Zion we return,

> Contending for our native heaven;
> That palace of our glorious King,
> We find it nearer while we sing.

And will you notice this? If you have spiritual discernment, whenever you meet a saint you become aware of two things about him. At one moment you feel "how natural and at-home he is" . . . and the next you say to yourself: "The man is an exile; he doesn't belong here at all."

You notice it in St. Paul. How busy he is for the kingdom in affairs of this world and then he sighs in my text to be "at home with the Lord."

That was how they always felt about Thomas Erskine of Linlathen. A friend tells me that, after his death, his life recurred to the memory of his old acquaintances like "the sigh of an exile. He seemed never to take root in this world. To him, many of the things that most interested other men were only the furniture of an inn, not really important; he wasn't *staying*. He was a wayfarer—a pilgrim." That is one of the authentic marks of the saint. He is "the pilgrim of an inward Odyssey." This earth, he knows, is not his place.

My friends, do *you* know that? I want to say to any poor, lost sinner within reach of my voice now: You may have lost your way, but don't lose your address. Don't deny that hunger in your soul. Don't say: It isn't there; earth satisfies me; when this life is over I will have had all that I want of life.

That, I notice, is what Logan Pearsall Smith says in his autobiography: "For any other form of being I feel no longing." He had lost the religion of his saintly mother. He never had a robust religion of his own. Then he denied the hunger for anything more. I say: He had not only lost his way; he had lost his address.

God keep you on your guard against that. The homesickness for God in your heart is a precious, divine gift. It won't make you less keen to serve your fellows here below, but it will be a constant reminder to you that the most permanent dwelling earth provides is a tent, and at any time the word may come to draw the pegs. We are, indeed, "strangers and pilgrims here below."

Your interest in heaven may expose you, of course, to the charge—even from fellow-Christians—of "otherworldliness." People who have made the "social gospel" the whole gospel are very free with that charge.

Ignore it!

You have been well taught that the interpretation of the Christian ethic in communal life is part of your plain business, but you know, and I know, that the only "new Jerusalem" *we* shall see is "not made with hands," but is "eternal in the heavens."

> Far o'er yon horizon
> Rise the City towers,
> Where our God abideth;
> That fair home is ours.

Here we sojourn; there we belong. You will work with zest, and skill, and thoroughness, in all that concerns the outworkings of God's purpose on this earth, and you will work the better because, by faith, you have the perfect always in view.

Only those people work with *full* effectiveness for the new Jerusalem below who see the new Jerusalem above. They make it after "the pattern which has been shown them in the mount."

Think of the glorious social consequences of the evangelistic work of John Wesley, and Lord Shaftesbury, and William Booth—all God-intoxicated men; all consciously marching to Zion; all sure of heaven.

Be sure of it yourself; it is where you *belong*.

> Send hope before to grasp it,
> Till hope be lost in sight.

Some time ago a poor drunkard came into this church and committed his life to Christ. Twenty years before he had been a church official in the Midlands, but he came to London, took to drink, and drifted to the gutter. When he capitulated to Christ he had a pathetic hope that his thirst might be quenched by some stroke of omnipotence. It wasn't.

There began on that day when he surrendered to our Lord a long guerrilla warfare in his soul between the deadly craving and the keeping power of Christ.

As his new friend, I suggested that, on any day in which he found the fight especially hard, he might drop in and we could have a prayer together. He dropped in quite often. His drawn face often told its own story. We would go into the little chapel at once and pray.

One day, as I was praying with him, he broke down completely. The contrast between his earlier life of holy service, and the revolting bestiality to which drunkenness had brought him, was too much. He sobbed like a child and said:

"I know I'm in the gutter. I know it. But Oh! . . . I don't belong there, do I? Tell me, I don't belong there. . . ."

I put my arm around him. I felt a great elation even in the embarrassment of his tears. He had lost his way . . . but not his address.

"No," I said quite positively, "you don't belong there. . . . You belong to God. At the last, *heaven is your home.*"

NOTES

The Heavenly Home

John Ker (1819–1886) is little known today, but in his day he was a respected preacher and professor of preaching and pastoral work at the United Free Church Seminary in Glasgow, Scotland. He published two volumes of sermons.

This one is from the *Sermons Second Series*, published in Edinburgh in 1888 by David Douglas.

John Ker

5

THE HEAVENLY HOME

In my Father's house are many mansions (John 14:2).

WE CANNOT READ the life of our Lord Jesus Christ in the Gospels without observing how it gathers and grows in intensity as it nears its end, that last great act of self-devotion when He is lifted up to draw all men unto Him. And there is a like progress in His words and manner of speech. Compare, for example, the Sermon on the Mount, its guidance for the practical Christian life, and its lessons from nature for confidence in God, with this discourse in the upper chamber at Jerusalem, and you feel the change. It is like that between the fresh meeting in the morning sunlight, with the day spread out before them, and the parting under the solemn shadows of the nightfall. We feel as if the voice must have sunk at times to whispers, but it has a depth and earnestness which it could never express before, because it had never found the season and the listeners. His soul is about to be poured out in death; His disciples have a dim feeling that such an end is at hand; and His heart is now opened in most tender pity to them for all they have to suffer when He shall be no longer in the midst of them. Such is the undertone which pervades the whole discourse. But while the earthly sun is sinking the stars are coming out in the sky, to tell of a grander universe, and of purposes beyond the narrow homes under whose roofs we now meet and part. Nowhere in any part of His teaching does our Lord point to these so distinctly, for as stars shine in the dark His hopes brighten amid life's shadows. There is not anywhere in all the Bible a view of the heavenly world so clear and full, and yet so brief and simple, as is contained in His opening words. It is like the firmament itself, "inlaid with patines of bright gold." We have, first, His description of heaven,

"In my Father's house are many mansions"; next, the assurance of it, "if it were not so, I would have told you"; then, the fitting up and furnishing of it, "I go to prepare a place for you"; still further, the safe conduct to it, "If I go and prepare a place for you, I will come again and receive you unto Myself"; and, last of all, the essence of it, "that where I am, there ye may be also."

We shall turn attention now to the first of these, that, if we are under the shadow of partings, as indeed we always are, we may, with the help of Christ's Spirit, share in the comforts He offers.

Heaven Is Characterized by Permanence

The first remark we make is that our Lord teaches us to connect with heaven the thought of *permanence*. It is a place of "mansions." Both the English word and the Greek intimate this a place where the dwellers shall abide, like a city to wanderers in the wilderness. "You have known Me," He says to His disciples, "for a few years, moving to and fro, but I leave you for the city of God, where you also shall enter in, to go out no more at all." The promise answers a very deep desire of the human heart. "All things change," the old heathen poet says, "and we with them."

But the change in things around us is like fixity to the change that is in ourselves. It may be that the earth and sun and stars and all material things are slowly moving from their old forms into new, their light paling, their vitality decaying, to be renewed we know not how; but their slow, stern cycles seem to us changeless when we think of ourselves. Let anyone who has advanced but a short way in life look around. Old times are away, old interests, old aims: the haunts, the friends, the faces of our youth, where are they? Gone, or so changed that we dare not think to recall them. Or, if we try, we cannot; they are so different, so far away, such a mist has come up from the stream of time that they are shadows dim and broken like things in a dream. And we are changing within. If we could keep up the life and freshness there, it would be less sad. But there are few who can say the spring leaves are as green, the flowers as sweet, the summer days as long and sunny, the heart as open and free from distrust, as when life was young. There is indeed compensation for this, if we will seek it. If we have a home in God through Christ, it brings in something better than youthful brightness, even a peace which flows like a river, a joy and gladness at times, the taste of which is like the wine of Christ's higher feast, that makes the guests say, "The new is better." But here, too, there is frequently change. The anchor of our hope seems to lose its hold, our sense of pardon and peace may be broken, and the face of God, if seen at all, may look dim and distant. The disciples who were in possession of this fellowship with Christ at the close of the week were, before another, scattered from around His cross, or hopelessly seeking Him in His grave.

It is from such changes that the promise of Christ carries us to a fixed place of abode. The permanence of the dwelling shall ensure permanence in all that belongs to the dwellers in it; otherwise the home and the inhabitants would be out of harmony. There must be, indeed, the change of progress; it is the permanence not of death but of life; and so the changes of decay, of loss, of bereavement, of the unreturning past, these are gone with the last great change, which ends the perishing and opens the eternal. There shall be no wavering of faith, no waning of hope, no chill of love. Faith shall see, and yet go on into the unseen; hope shall enjoy, and yet look forward; love shall be perfect, and yet have increase. Here, change at every step leaves some lost good behind it; there, change shall take all its good things forward into fuller possession, and thus become a growing permanence. Many a heart has said with David, "O that I had wings like a dove! for then would I fly away and be at rest"; and has found it no more in the solitude than in the city; but the hand that is put out at the window of this ark of refuge will ensure to it peace always, by all means. "There remaineth a rest to the people of God." We can rely on nothing else but His promise for the fulfillment of it. Sometimes it looks so strange, so unearthly, so utterly away from all the laws of nature and life as we see them here, that it seems incredible. We stand before Him like Nicodemus—"How can these things be?" In what part of this changing universe, by what reconstruction of this unstable soul? He has the same reply: "No man hath ascended up to heaven, but He that came down from heaven, even the Son of man, which is in heaven." It admits of none other; it is for faith, not for sight; for the trust of the heart, not for the telescope of science. If God has given us spirits that cry out for such a home, and if Christ has given us one fixed point in God's love, we can commit all the rest to Him. He who can create a spark of love in a human heart, which all the floods of change cannot quench, can raise it to a sun that shall no more go down. Heaven is a state before it is a place. It is being in God, then with God. The locality will flow from the heart. The way to be sure of a permanent home is to keep fast hold of Him who is the same yesterday, today, and forever.

Heaven Is Characterized by Extent and Variety

Our Lord teaches us to connect with heaven the thought of *extent and variety*. It has "many" mansions. This saying gains wonderful grandeur when we think of where it was spoken. The humble chamber where He and his friends are met is to be exchanged for a palace where there shall be room for them and all who shall believe on Him through their word—for the children of God scattered abroad from the beginning to the end of time. We narrow the walls of these final abodes in our imaginations as well as our hearts, but both Scripture and reason give us conceptions of their vastness that widen to the infinite. Our present life is related to it as that of childhood to manhood. Let us think of the dwelling of the child, where it looks from its little window on the few houses or fields which make up its world, and then let us compare it with what the man knows of his present world-residence, when he has surveyed with his eye or his mind the breadth of the earth with its oceans and lands that stretch over continents by Alps and Andes. The difference, we may well believe, is not so great as that between childhood here and manhood there. Let us think, moreover, of the way in which the Bible speaks of the inhabitants; for we can judge of a city as we look on the roads and multitudes that make it their center. There is indeed but one gate: "No man cometh unto the Father but by Me." Yet by it there passes in "a multitude which no man can number, out of every kindred and tongue and people and nation." It is a heart-reviving thing when we can feel sure that numbers without number have entered consciously by that wide door, reading over it His own handwriting, "Him that cometh unto Me, I will in no wise cast out"; and joyfully singing, as they pass through, "This is the gate of God." But there enter at the wicket-gate Christiana and also the children, many Ready-to-halts and Feeble-minds, and far-off pilgrims for whom we can find no names, but who are written in the Lamb's Book of Life. Infants are carried through the door sleeping, who wake up in the heavenly city to read their deliverance first in the face of their Deliverer; and it is not for us to say by what far-off rays in dark nights, by what doubtful paths amid many imperfections, hearts have been yearning to this home. There have been Simeons and Annas outside the temple waiting for the consolation; and to desire and wait is, with Christ, to reach the door. The notices of Rahab and Ruth, of Ittai and Naaman, of the wise men of the East, and the Greeks who came up to the Passover, of the Ethiopian eunuch and the devout Cornelius, are hints for the enlargement of our hopes about many who had the same yearning in their hearts, though they did not see the walls of any earthly Jerusalem. And, if we believe the Bible, there are long eras to run, when the flow shall be toward God more than it ever has been away from Him. Though it seems at times, when great material conquests are gained, as if the soul were depressed and almost crushed out under its own discoveries, it must awake to its true birthright in the spiritual and divine. The ages of faith are not behind us, they are before; for we can never be persuaded that the world's advance is to the gulf of despair. From many sides and in different ways, from regions of the shadow of death and from realms of light, Christ will gather inhabitants to the final dwelling place, and make good the assurance that He shall see of the travail of His soul, that He shall bring many sons unto glory, and be so satisfied in His works that He shall call on His universe to join in the satisfaction—"Be ye glad and rejoice forever in that which I create: for, behold, I create Jerusalem a rejoicing, and her people a joy." And then we have to think, with all this, that there are to be other inhabitants. From the beginning of Scripture to the end, we have glimpses of spiritual beings, other than human beings, who serve God in carrying out His purposes in this world, and who are to be joined with us at last in work and fellowship. There is to be a gathering together of all things in Christ, and the holy angels have relations to Him which will give them their share in His home. When we think of this, how the extent of the heavenly world grows!—mansions which shall contain the innumerable company of angels and the myriads of saved men, where they shall have room to expatiate and be at large! It is not well for us to attempt a premature union between the discoveries of material science and the revelations of God's Word—or to say that in some particular sphere of the firmament, near or far, the mansions may be forming; yet the discoveries of science may help us to extend our hopes. When the astronomer's glass shows us worlds on worlds, suns of systems and systems of suns spread through the sky, under whose magnitude and distances imagination faints, we may feel it not presumptuous to expect that He who has done so much for the temporary lodgment, so to speak, of His intelligent creatures will have at least something corresponding for their final residence. And if in the history of this world, from the rude inorganic mass up to present forms of life and thought, we can see every epoch bringing forth something more allied to spirit, may we not trust that this world does not show us the close, but that other forms higher and more akin to spirit will be found extending beyond these, or growing up through their ruins? In some way, we may be sure, there will be abodes for the inhabitants, suited to their number and character and wants.

But this promise of many mansions holds out the prospect of *variety* as well as extent. In all God's works the many means the manifold. When we visit new lands we expect new forms of life. There is no tame monotony anywhere in the world which is our present residence, and doubtless the creative power, which shows itself so exhaustless in its diversified operations here, will continue to work through infinite space and infinite time on this same plan. It suits itself to the wants of man's nature—may we not say the nature of all intelligence, which must have the new as well as the old. The divine Wisdom, who has His delights with the sons of men, had an eternity in the past, "ere ever the earth was"; but He has His coming eternity when He shall make glad the city of God with fresh and ever-growing streams of knowledge. Let us not think, then, of the mansions as copies of one another, but as giving endless room to all the faculties of God's intelligent creatures in the study of His works and ways. It is to indicate this that those who stand on the sea of glass mingled with fire are spoken of as singing the new song, which has its grand parallel in God's doings in space and time: "Great and marvelous are thy works, Lord God Almighty; just and true are thy ways, Thou King of saints."

Heaven Is Characterized by Unity

Our Lord further teaches us to connect with the heavenly world the thought of *unity*. It is "a house" of many mansions. The extent and variety of the mansions of the great future would leave us still unsatisfied, would fill us even with perplexity and fear, unless there were a center holding them together, and bringing them close to our hearts. These abodes of the future, manifold as they are, have walls around, and an over-arching roof which make them one house, and that house a home. It will be a world of expanse for thought and action, but a world also for musing and meditation; where, as in Isaiah's vision, the wings may be spread for flight, or folded on the feet for quiet waiting, or covering the face for inward contemplation. To some this last may be the most attractive, but for all holy desires there will be a provision; many mansions, and yet a home.

There is a thought implied which to many hearts may be not less dear. The chambers of a house have their communication with one another, and the heavenly world,

wide as it is, shall have a unity of fellowship. In the
present world the children of God are far apart. We speak
of the one family in heaven and earth, but it is of faith not
of sight, seldom even of feeling. It is a multitude of pilgrims broken up into little bands which never meet or
overtake each other in this world. The word that passes
along their ranks is, "Here we have no continuing city:
we seek one to come." The little bands themselves are
separated by the emergencies of life, by inevitable death,
and, what is still more painful, by misunderstandings
and prejudices, by chills of heart and jealousies; and
they rear their many little mansions, forgetful of the one
house. The word of the Savior promises a reversal of this
long, sad history. The barriers of time and space are to be
withdrawn, and all who have been and shall be the friends
of God brought together for mutual knowledge and blessed
converse. The family above, the unfallen and the restored,
the innumerable company of angels and spirits of just
men made perfect, shall be joined by the family below,
and the Jordan dried up, never to overflow its bed again.
How the wide dwellings spread through God's universe
shall be brought together in friendship, we cannot conjecture, but in some way there shall be one great palace
home, and "the Lord shall be king, and his name one." As
we try to realize it, our thoughts pass along the scenes in
Scripture, where heaven bends down to meet earth, and
give us glimpses of this coming union; the vision of Jacob,
when he saw the angels of God, and called the place God's
house; the time when "God shined from Paran, and came
with ten thousands of his saints, when He loved the
people, and they sat down at his feet"; the scene on the
mount, when the disciples would have built tabernacles
that their Master and Moses and Elias might remain
there and hold converse in their hearing; the sitting down
with Abraham and Isaac and Jacob in the kingdom of
God; the coming to Mount Zion and the heavenly Jerusalem and all the glorious dwellers whom the apostle ranges
rank within rank, till he comes to the Leader and Commander of them, Jesus, the Mediator of the new covenant. To meet in one home with all the best in God's

universe, to see them, listen to them, speak with them, to pass from chamber to chamber, from age to age and world to world, to learn the secrets deep buried in the past, and brood on still undisclosed depths in the future—this will be part of the unity of the heavenly home. Peter, when delivered from prison by the angel, seems to have recognized fully what God had done for him only when he was brought into the company of his brethren; and there are poor sufferers around us confined to the sickbed and the solitude of their own thoughts, with none but God to bear them company, for whom the dreary loneliness of life shall be first broken in the enjoyment of this fellowship. "They shall be brought out of prison to praise God's name."

And yet there is a hope in the friendship of the house which comes closer to the heart. We have never seen these elder-born of the family, and we have never lost them. But there are those who have left empty places in hearts and homes, which can never be filled while life lasts. There are children newly gone, and fathers and mothers far away—some for whom the heart is sore in the busy daytime, and some who come back in visions of the night with strange and inexpressible sadness. The house Christ speaks of has rooms where He keeps His friends safe against a time of meeting. "Them that sleep in Jesus will God bring with Him"; and this makes the promise of His return a consolation to the bereaved: "I will see you again, and your heart shall rejoice, and your joy no man taketh from you." There are views of the future world for the mind of man in its activities, its pursuit of noble aims and lofty ideals—counterparts of what in this world we call philosophy and poetry, which must have their place there if man is still to study God's plans, and rejoice in His works; but these would be cold in their height and grandeur without trustful repose for the heart in human affection; and as it is said of God in this world, "The day is thine, the night also is thine," we may believe that there too He has provided for souls their period of rest, and that there also "man shall go forth unto his work and to his labor until the evening"; to find in some way that, while the mind has its world, the heart has its home.

Heaven Is a Paternal Home

But something is needed to secure this, and our Lord teaches us to carry to the thought of heaven a *filial heart*. It is *the Father's* house, a paternal home. This is needed to make it a home in any sense; needed to give the heart rest either on earth or in heaven. Men who inquire into the facts and laws of the world, and find no God in it, have made themselves homeless. Men who have found human affection, but no God beneath it, have found only the shadow of a home. Thought and affection are shallow, short-lived things without Him who sets the solitary in families—the Father of spirits. It is to teach us this that God has made a father's love the bond of a true human household. You recollect how Joseph, when he spoke with his brethren and asked them of their welfare, could not rest until he had drawn an answer to his question, "Is your father well, the old man of whom ye spake? Is he yet alive?" And when the hope of seeing him was near, how he made ready his chariot, and went up to meet Israel his father, and fell on his neck and wept; and Israel said unto Joseph, "Now let me die, since I have seen thy face, because thou art yet alive." We may feel sure that the restored affection of his brethren, even Benjamin's, could not have filled the place in his heart had his father been no more; and the good of the land of Egypt would have been empty, and its glory gone, without his father to look on and share it with him. It is not that love like this leads us, as some would say, to think of having a Father in God; God Himself, desiring to be our Father, has put this love into our hearts, that it may reflect His own. It does not begin below, but is a gift which comes from above from the Father of lights. Let a soul but once awake truly to the feeling of its misery, if it is orphaned in the universe, no pitying eye looking down on its solitude, no hand to guide its wanderings or hold it up in its weakness, no infinite heart to which it can bring its own when wounded and bleeding, let it see or think it sees that the world is fatherless, and that there is no hope beyond the grave for those that are broken in their hearts and grieved in their minds, and I cannot understand how that soul should not be smitten with despair. If it were possible to enter heaven and find no Father there, heaven would be the grave of hope. The soul might search its many mansions, as Mary sought Christ's grave, and when it found no God it would stand without the door weeping as before an empty sepulcher. To cry for Him and hear no answer, would be, in the words of Richter's dream, "to listen only to the eternal storm, which no one governs; to look to the immeasurable firmament for a divine eye, and to meet a black, bottomless socket"; and then the soul might choose "strangling and death rather than life." But what will make the heavenly house a home is that it will have, not friends and brethren only, but a Father, whose presence will fill it, and make itself felt in every pulse of every heart.

If we were to think of every mansion in it having its four enclosing walls, each would have its inscription written by God's own hand. There are those who have often doubted their acceptance and forgiveness, who have walked in darkness and with difficulty stayed themselves on God, questioning whether they might not in the end be castaways; and it stands inscribed, "Thy sins which are many are forgiven thee." There are those who have felt the want of the likeness they should bear to God, and of the love of gratitude which should bestow it on them. They take home to themselves the reproach, "Their spot is not the spot of his children: is not he thy Father that hath bought thee?" For them it is written, "Ye backsliding children, I will heal your backslidings." "And they shall see his face, and his name shall be on their foreheads." There are those who have felt all through life as if God were turned to be their enemy, and were fighting against them. Their desires have been thwarted, their hearts pierced through and through with losses and crosses and cruel wounds, and failure upon failure has followed their plans. But it is written, "Whom the Lord loveth He correcteth, even as a father the son in whom he delighteth"; and under it, "All things work together for good to them that love God." And there are those who have yearnings of heart to feel God's presence close and constant, to hear Him and speak with Him, and be sure He is not, as some would say to them, a voice or a vision or a dream of their fond imagination. They have felt it at times so certain that they could say, "The Lord is the strength of my life; of whom shall I be afraid?" But clouds roll in on the assurance, and the voice seems far off or silent, as if it were among the trees of the garden; and it is toward evening, and there is doubt and fear. But it shall be "as the light of the morning, when the sun riseth, even a morning without clouds; as the tender grass springing out of the earth by clear shining after rain"; and His name shall be written as the "Father of lights, with whom is no variableness, neither shadow of turning." And he who reads it shall say, "Thou art my Father, my God, and the rock of my salvation." Here is hope and aim for stricken spirits and solitary hearts. There is a Father, there is a home. The sky is not empty, the world is not orphaned. "Doubtless Thou art our Father, our Redeemer."

Heaven Is Christ's Dwelling

Our Lord has taught us to connect heaven with the thought of *Himself*—"My" Father's house. Heaven is the house of Christ's Father. It is as when an arch is built, and last the keystone is put in which binds it all into one; or as when a palace has been raised with all its rooms and their furniture complete, but it is dark or dimly seen by lights carried from place to place. The sun arises, and by the central dome the light is poured into all the corridors and chambers, and by the windows there are prospects over hill and valley and river. The Lord Jesus Christ is the sun of this house. If we think of its mansions, and wonder where the final resting place shall be, it is where Christ takes up His dwelling. His person is the place of heaven— "that they may be with Me where I am." If we think of its extent and variety, our imaginations might be bewildered, and our souls chilled by boundless fields of knowledge, which stir the intellect and famish the heart; but where He is, knowledge becomes the wisdom of love—the daylight softened; and a heart beats in the universe which throbs to its remotest and minutest fiber; for "in Him is life, and the life is the light of men." If we think of heaven in its unity of fellowship, it is in Him that it is maintained and felt—at His throne, through His love—according to His prayer,

"That they all may be one, as Thou, Father, art in Me, and I in Thee, that they also may be one in us." And if we think of a Father in heaven, it is Christ who has revealed Him. "No man hath seen God at any time; the only-begotten Son, which is in the bosom of the Father, He hath declared Him." Even in heaven, God cannot be seen by created eye; the pure in heart see Him, but with the heart. For the human eye, it is Jesus Christ, the glorified God-man, who says in heaven as on earth, "He that hath seen Me hath seen the Father." He who gave us a corporeal nature, and surrounded us with a material world, has put into us the craving wish to approach Him with our entire beings, soul, body, and spirit, and He has met the wish in the Son of God. In His person are enshrined the infinite attributes of God, so that finite creatures can look on them, and apprehend them, and see the Father in the Son. Thus God becomes open to human vision, and accessible to human affection.

But beyond all this, it is Christ's Father's house because He is the way and the door to it. "No man," He Himself has said, "cometh unto the Father, but by Me." I know not of any heaven for men but that which the Lord Jesus has opened up and fitted and filled, and I know of no Father for them but the God and Father of our Lord and Savior Jesus Christ. None will ever reach it, dim as their sight has been, and broken the twilight of their groping, but it shall be found that His foot led the way, and His hand upheld their goings. Even those who needed not redemption, who were born and have remained children of the family, shall have their knowledge and happiness increased by this, that they are in Christ's Father's house. They are adopted into it, though it be by another adoption than ours; and when they worship before the throne it is for them also the throne of a Lamb as it had been slain. It is because it is Christ's Father's house that new songs have been made for it, and a new and peculiar joy created, joy among the angels for sinners that repent, joy among the saved that they have had wonderful deliverance, and joy in the heart of the Father Himself—"This my son was dead, and is alive again; he was lost, and is found." It is this which gives its deepest and highest meaning to the heaven of the gospel; it is the heaven of the Redeemer—"Where sin abounded, grace does much more abound." It is as if from the lava of a crater there should break a stream of water to heal and purify; "to give beauty for ashes and the oil of joy for mourning"; and to recover from the waste of sin a new heaven and a new earth, in which righteousness shall dwell.

Heaven's Door Is Open

And yet this truth, that the heavenly house has for its center the throne and cross of Christ, that it is the home of the pardoned and purified, makes it needful that a closing word should be spoken to be pondered by us all. Are you on the way to it, are you preparing for it? It is surely the most reasonable of all things to believe that a man cannot dwell in peace in God's house, unless he is at peace with God Himself and that he cannot enjoy the heaven of Christ without the mind of Christ. God cannot make a man blessed by surrounding him with blessings. He cannot give him heaven, if the man will not have God Himself. If, then, you are refusing God, you are refusing God's heaven; if you will not have Him in your heart, you can never look with loving confidence upon His face. All deceptive dreams, all vain illusion about what God may do, are scattered by this, that God has set heaven's door open to you, and you will not enter it; you are framing a heart and life within you which make misery sure by the most fixed of all laws, the law of the divine nature. It is for you to ponder this now. If you will but bethink yourself, He who has made heaven ready, and who is the door to it, is now at the door of your heart, ready to enter with pardon for all the past, and divine help for all the future. Will you not receive Him? "Lord, I am not worthy that You should come under my roof; but I bid You welcome; take Your place, fill every mansion of my soul, grant me a sense of Your presence in the peace You give, the peace that is Your own, and then I shall know there is a heaven reserved for me, and that I shall be kept for it by the power of God through faith unto salvation."

NOTES

The Door to Heaven

George W. Truett (1867–1944) was perhaps the best-known Southern Baptist preacher of his day. He pastored the First Baptist Church of Dallas, Texas, from 1897 until his death and saw it grow both in size and influence. Active in denominational ministry, Truett served as president of the Southern Baptist Convention and for five years was president of the Baptist World Alliance, but he was known primarily as a gifted preacher and evangelist. Nearly a dozen books of his sermons were published.

This sermon was taken from *The Salt of the Earth* published in 1949 by Broadman Press.

George W. Truett

6

THE DOOR TO HEAVEN

After this I looked, and behold, a door was opened in heaven (Revelation 4:1).

YOU AT ONCE recognize our text as the words of the Apostle John who was banished to the Isle of Patmos because of his fealty to Christ. On this island, there were given unto him visions and revelations of God and of the eternal glory probably beyond those ever vouchsafed to any other person in the flesh. John seems to have been greatly loved by Jesus. You remember that on one occasion John leaned his head on Jesus' breast. On that island, with all its isolation and loneliness, wonderful visions were given John of Christ and the glory above. He recounted in the Scripture a number of things he had seen, and then said: "After this, I looked, and behold, a door was opened in heaven."

We do not know much about heaven, and all that we do know is revealed to us here in the Bible. This is the sure word of prophecy, and we are not following cunningly devised fables when we follow this sure word of the long centuries. The only clear teacher concerning the life beyond was Jesus. All else has largely been guesswork and speculation, except as the Holy Spirit inspired certain writers to set down in the Bible glimpses concerning the world beyond. We do not know about the world to come, but we do know some things by intimations, by glimpses, and by certain point-blank statements that Christ Himself made.

The awful things we know about hell are things told us by Jesus. I will not flout His teaching, plain as sunlight, clear as words can make it, that there is an eternal difference between the man who accepts Christ as his personal Savior and the man who rejects Him. Christ is the only clear teacher as to that great truth. And He is the one clear and informed teacher about the fact of heaven.

In dark and challenging days like these through which we are passing, we do well to rest our hearts by frequently letting our thoughts dwell on the revelations we have as to the reality and blessedness of heaven. Long ago the devout Jew had an expression strikingly significant: "Let Jerusalem come into your mind." And no matter where the Jew went, nor what his battles and burdens, nor what the pressure upon him, that expression summoned him, inspired him, aroused him, challenged him, cheered him. "Let Jerusalem come into your mind." So should we let the heavenly Jerusalem come often into our minds. As we go our ways, with our battles and tasks and questions and responsibilities, often we need to pause and earnestly ponder the fact of the heavenly Jerusalem which Christ has arranged for His friends.

Heaven Is a Place

What does the Bible teach us about heaven? Several answers are available. Let us glance at them briefly this hour. For one thing, it teaches that heaven is *a place*. There is a great deal of loose talking about heaven being merely a state, merely an abstraction, merely an idea. Jesus teaches that heaven is a place. One may say that patriotism is a mere abstraction, but if there is not a country in which people may live and upon which they may bestow their love, then there would be no patriotism. Heaven is not merely a state. It is that, but it is so much more than that! Heaven is a place, and the Bible sets forth that fact in words clear and unmistakable, again and again.

Heaven is called *a house*. Jesus says: "In my Father's house are many mansions; if it were not so, I would have told you. I go to prepare a place for you. And if I go and prepare a place for you, I will come again, and receive you unto myself, that where I am, there ye may be also." And in another place, heaven is called *a city*—"the city which has foundations, whose builder and maker is God." And John here in the last book of the New Testament in words glowing and glorious gives us an earthly description of that marvelous place called heaven.

What Kind of Place Is Heaven?

What kind of a place is it? It is a holy place. That truth should delight our hearts as we aspire after purity, holiness and righteousness unalloyed! I think that of all the glimpses I have had here in this Book of that world where Christ shall gather His friends to be with Himself forever, to my own heart the most ravishing of all the pictures of heaven is that it is to be a place where nothing that defiles shall ever come. Oh, at last to be holy and to be perfect even as God is holy and perfect! Nothing that defiles shall enter heaven. Nothing that is unclean, unholy, impure, unchaste, shall ever cast its black shadow athwart that world of love above. Heaven then is to be a holy place. Here we have warfare because of dual personality. We have the flesh warring against the spirit, and the spirit warring against the flesh. We often cry out: "Who shall deliver me from this dead body?" We are delivered, by and by, from all that defiles and pollutes. The friends of Christ are destined for a place perfect in its righteousness.

What kind of a place is heaven? Heaven is to be a *busy* place. His servants shall serve Him, we are told here in this Book. Have you ever tried to think what that service will be? Can you not imagine yourself on eagle's wings, flying through infinite space, when you get home to be with Christ? You see this planet on which we live is relatively a very small place—twenty-five thousand miles around it, they tell us, and yet a speck in God's universe. Yonder, in the immeasurable and infinite immensities of the eternal spaces of God, are worlds and worlds and worlds—worlds by the million, it may be. And it may be that one of the services on which He will send us, when we come to the cloudless, sinless, perfect land is to go here and there, not limited as we are now, and declare the riches and wonders and glories of God, as we can never declare them while we are here fettered in the flesh. His servants shall serve Him. Give fancy free rein when you think about the unalloyed, the unlimited, the immeasurable service which throughout the ages eternal we are to render when we get to yonder land.

Have you thought that He may send us forth as missionaries to proclaim salvation to unknown multitudes who sit in spiritual darkness? How I should like to go, leading this great church family from this height to that, from this place to that, to say: "We have tasted of the riches of the glory of God, for when a baleful thing went out to the earth and put the shadow of its black wings upon us, and smote us to death, the name of which awful thing was sin, God sent His only begotten Son to come to earth and die for us, and we believed on Him, and He made us victors even over sin."

A busy place heaven is to be, without any weariness. Here we are wearied. Oh, the pressure of life's battle is such, the work to be done is such, the call is such, that the brain gets tired, the head bows with weariness, the limbs drag with burdens, and the spirit cries out its pain because of exhaustion. There shall be none of that in God's house above.

One day I visited at the cottage of a seamstress of our church family, who was very, very poor, fighting then a hard battle for herself and her children. She is now in the better land, where the battles do not wear and tear the flesh any more. I said to her, as she sewed away busily: "What feature of heaven appeals most to you, my friend?" And the tears came in a rush to her tired eyes, as she laid down her sewing and said: "Oh, sir, the feature of heaven that most delights me is that some day I shall rest. I am tired all the time. You see, I sew until late in the night, to get food for these children, and I get up early in the morning, and by the early light I sew for my children. I have sewed until my fingers are bloodless. Oh, sir, in heaven I shall rest and the weariness and the pain of this body of mine will be gone forever." Bless her precious memory! She will rest, and she does rest.

> There I shall bathe my wearied soul
> In seas of heavenly rest,
> And not one wave of trouble roll
> Across my peaceful breast.

There will be rest for the weary, in the sense that no weariness, no drudgery, no burden shall ever be felt in heaven by us for one moment.

What kind of a place is heaven? Heaven is a populous place. Oh, there will be many people in heaven. A man asked Jesus: "Will there be few saved?" Well, now that is not a practical question to ask Jesus. He turned and said to him: "Strive to enter in at the strait gate." He said a stronger word than that. He said: "Agonize to enter in at the strait gate." Do not ask a speculative question like that. Be sure of getting there yourself. How wisely and instructively Jesus answered the numerous questions asked Him. But the Bible does tell us that heaven is to be a populous place. Oh, the children that will be there! I like to fancy them playing, as in the streets of a city, where no auto will crush them. Oh, the children that shall be in that cloudless land! All of the blessed little fellows, who die before they can discern between right and wrong, before they can discriminate, before they can pass morally and personally on the question of the call of God to repentance and faith—all of them dying this side that line of personal accountability, every one, shall pass through the gates into the city of God.

That doctrine once preached by some that there would be infants in hell is a doctrine of devils. It is not taught in the Word of God. It is nowhere hinted at in the Word of God. But the Word of God, with a breadth of mercy like the wideness of the sea, indicates for us clearly that these blessed children, dying this side that age of personal accountability, shall every one be carried into the realms of the blessed forever. Will it not be glorious to see the children there?

And then, oh, the multitudes of adults who shall be there! Down the long ages, even from before Abraham's time, there have been those who looked toward the coming of the Messiah, and then for these nineteen centuries, millions untold have looked backward at the fulfillment of their hope in the coming of that Messiah, the Deliverer, the Light of the world, the Refuge for the oppressed, the Redeemer of the sinful and lost. Oh, the hosts that shall be there, who believe on Christ! John, this same John said: "I looked and saw a great multitude," through that open door of heaven, which was flung ajar for him one day, in his loneliness, on the Isle of Patmos. He "looked and beheld a great multitude, which no man could number," and they were gathered out of every tribe, and kindred and tongue and people in all the world. Blessed be God, there will be many in heaven. I do not believe that hell shall have a majority at all, not at all, not at all. What a host, illimitable, immeasurable, shall be yonder in that blessed land! A populous place heaven is to be.

What else about heaven? The Bible has another word for us. Heaven is to be a perfectly *happy* place. Read John's description here in the last book—glimpse after glimpse. "There shall be no night there." Night is the symbol of sorrow. Night carries with it terror. In the night we are afraid. In the night the children cry out in their fear for the touch of hand, for the voice of a father or mother. In the night the sick one wearily longs for the light of the morning. "There shall be no night there." "They need no candle, neither light of the sun." Christ, the Light of the world shall Himself be the light in that world beyond. No night, no pain, no tears, no suffering, no sorrow, no death shall ever enter that happy place called heaven.

Would you not like to go to a land where there is no death? I came back just a little while ago from one of our young men, ill with pneumonia, whose life hangs in the balance. The doctor said: "It looks like any five minutes may be the last." The young wife, in her desperate grief, asked as I left to come to this service: "Why is this? Why is this?" All I could do was try to turn her thoughts to a land where death shall never come.

O Death, you are an enemy to the race! What do you care for the blessed babe? What do you care? You take it out of the hands of love and carry it away, and though they cover the body with flowers, yet it is dead, and to the grave it must go. What do you care that a little woman go robed in widow's weeds, battling in loneliness to the last? What do you care for her, O Death? No respecter of persons are you! Blessed be God, yonder is a land where no hearse shall pause at any cottage in God's fair country. Yonder is a land where no crepe will ever be seen on any door. Yonder is a land where no physician nor kindly nurse shall ever be needed. All the conditions of life are perfect forever. I do not wonder that Ponce de Leon was happy in the thought that he had found the fountain of youth. Yonder is a land where people never grow old. Infinite in blessedness! That is heaven!

What else? Heaven is our real *home*. Oh, that comes close to us. Heaven is to be our home, our final, permanent, eternal home. "They shall go out no more forever," is what Jesus promised. That is home. This is not our home. We are strangers and pilgrims here.

I am a pilgrim, I am a stranger,
I can tarry, I can tarry but a night.

Our tents shall soon be folded. Heaven is our home. "I go to prepare a place for you," said Jesus. Be not agitated. This is not your home at all. You are camped here for a few hours, and the camp must soon be broken up and you must move home. Oh, the melody in the word *home*! There is music and sweetness immeasurable in the word *home*!

The man with his small salary, struggling to make ends meet for himself and his wife and several little children, says: "What does it matter? The children will have their little faces at the window when I come home tonight, waiting to welcome me, believing that I am the finest man earth ever saw, and that beats all of the money in the world." That is home. There the wife, with a trust that would make an angel look on with a smile of infinite blessedness, says: "This man is dearer to me than all the earth beside." That is home, that is the right kind of wedded love. That is where the children ask: "Did anybody ever have such a daddy and mother as we have?" Yes, that is an earthly home. But, alas, how quickly the scene can change. How quickly the clouds can come down with their blackness and empty their fearful fury on defenseless heads, and that home be shattered and despoiled. This world is not our real home. Heaven is that. Cloudless, blessed forever! No sorrow nor disappointment nor death can enter there.

Not long ago, a boy from Georgia was slowly dying in a Dallas hospital. He kept saying to me, as I visited him repeatedly: "If I could just get back to the old home in Georgia!" I wrote his father and said: "Edgar's case is incurable. He wants to die at home." Soon the plain old farmer came across the long miles from Georgia. I did all I could to help and comfort that fine old father who tenderly tried to be mother and nurse and doctor, all through the long train journey from Dallas to Georgia. As they were leaving I said: "Write me about it when you get home."

In about a week after he reached home, I had his letter saying: "We have just come from Edgar's funeral. As we neared home, we propped him on pillows in the carriage which brought us from the railroad station across the hills and the mountains. When he got in sight of his old home here among the trees, he did his best to shout; and when at last he was in the home and mother had kissed him, and the sisters and brothers had kissed him, he said: 'I can die in perfect peace, because I am at home.'" Oh my soul, how sweet it will be at last to be at home! As the shades of night are lowered about us, we parents have a way of saying: "Are they all in? Are our loved ones all in? Is anyone near and dear to us absent?" Oh, to have reunited homes when we cross the tides separating us and the other world!

Are You on the Road to Heaven?

I have just one more word. Are you on the road that leads home to heaven? You should be altogether sure about that. There ought not to be guesswork about that. Are you on that road to heaven? There is just one road, just one. The Italians have a way of saying: "All roads lead to Rome." All roads lead to Rome—all roads. There is just one, my fellow men, that leads to heaven. My authority for that statement is Jesus, and His word is as clear as light. Thomas said unto Him, "Lord, how can we know the way? You are leaving us, and you are saying to us as you go, 'You know the way that I am going' and I answer, How can we know the way? Oh tell us the way, ere you leave us for good." Jesus replied: "I am the way, the truth and the life. No man cometh unto the Father, but by me." And He also said: "I am the door. By me, by me, if any man enter in, he shall be saved. He that climbeth up some other way is a thief and a robber."

You cannot steal your way into that blessed world. You cannot buy your way into heaven. Salvation which Christ gives is without money and without price. It is of Christ, free and full and sufficient, God's own grace, in Christ Jesus the Savior. Have you believed on Him as your Savior? Have you turned your case over to Christ? He is the great Physician for the soul, and none other can suffice. Priests cannot, and preachers cannot, and the pope cannot, and the church cannot.

> Other refuge have I none,
> Hangs my helpless soul on Christ.

He is all the refuge I want. I spurn the rest

O Church, I love you as I love no other institution in all the earth. Christ's masterpiece is the church. I am not depending on the church one iota to get me to heaven. O Baptism, beautiful symbol of the burial and resurrection of our glorious Lord, I delight in you, but I am not depending one iota on baptismal waters to get me to the land above the stars. Oh, good men all about me, whose fellowship is sweet, and whose counsels priceless, I treasure them all, but there is just one door to heaven and that door is Christ Jesus. Have you chosen that door? Have you put your case in His hands? "He that believeth on me hath everlasting life. He that believeth not is condemned already." Have you believed on Jesus?

Yonder at Gettysburg an army surgeon came back at the close of the battle looking for the wounded and suffering, and he found the dead on every side. He rode his horse, looking to see if somebody was still living unto whom he could minister. Presently he saw a man down in a little trench, lying on his back. The army surgeon reined up his horse and looked at the man and said. "I am too late. He is evidently gone." But as he said that to himself, a smile played around the lips of that dying soldier. The army surgeon dismounted and knelt down by him. Every minute or two that smile played upon those dying lips, and every time the smile came, the lips parted, and one little word was whispered and that word was: "Here!" "Here!" "Here!" Then the surgeon shook the soldier gently, if haply he might rouse him to consciousness of earthly things, and succeeded. The surgeon said: "Why are you saying 'Here'?" And with faint whispers he said: "Oh, Doctor, they were calling the roll in heaven and I was answering to my name, for long ago, I gave my heart to Christ."

Here tonight, if they called the roll, would you say: "Here"? I would. God knows I would hurry to say it! Oh, if they called roll tonight for eternal issues, would you answer: "Lord Jesus, You know all things. You know that I love You, and You know that I have put my trust in You as my Savior forever."

> My hope is built on nothing less
> Than Jesus' blood and righteousness:
> I dare not trust the sweetest frame,
> But wholly lean on Jesus' name.
> On Christ, the Solid Rock I stand;
> All other ground is sinking sand.

There is one door to heaven and that door is Christ. Have you chosen that door? Are you trusting in Christ as the Savior of your soul for this world and for the next? Does your heart say: "Sir, I am?" Everyone whose heart says: "I am trusting my case to Christ for time and eternity," stand to your feet.

Oh, that is a great company. Are there those here who say: "I cannot stand on that, but I can tell you that I want that Savior for mine before it is too late. I wish you, O preacher, and you, O Christians, who speak with God, would offer one prayer for me, that I may not miss entrance into that door, that I may not miss the way of life"? Do you say: "I can go that far"? You stand with us, God bless you! God bless you, all. Let us pray.

NOTES

Many Mansions

Alexander Maclaren (1826–1910) was one of Great Britain's most famous preachers. While pastoring the Union Chapel, Manchester (1858–1903), he became known as "the prince of expository preachers." Rarely active in denominational or civic affairs, Maclaren invested his time in studying the Word in the original and sharing its truths with others in sermons that are still models of effective expository preaching. He published a number of books of sermons and climaxed his ministry by publishing his monumental *Expositions of Holy Scripture*.

This message is taken from his *Expositions,* Baker Book House reprint edition, Volume 10.

Alexander Maclaren

7

MANY MANSIONS

In My Father's house are many mansions: if it were not so, I would have told you (John 14:2).

SORROW NEEDS SIMPLE words for its consolation; and simple words are the best clothing for the largest truths. These eleven poor men were crushed and desolate at the thought of Christ's going; they fancied that if He left them they lost Him. And so, in simple, childlike words, which the weakest could grasp, and in which the most troubled could find peace, He said to them, after having encouraged their trust in Him, "There is plenty of room for you as well as for Me where I am going; and the frankness of our intercourse in the past might make you sure that if I were going to leave you I would have told you all about it. Did I ever hide from you anything that was painful? Did I ever allure you to follow Me by false promises? Would I have kept silence about it if our separation was to be final?" So, simply, as a mother might hush her babe upon her breast, He soothes their sorrow. And yet, in the quiet words, so level to the lowest apprehension, there lie great truths, far deeper than we yet have appreciated, and which will unfold themselves in their majesty and their greatness through eternity. "In My Father's house are many mansions; if it were not so, I would have told you."

Heaven Is the Father's House

Now note in these words, first, the *Father's house*, and its ample room.

There is only one other occasion recorded in which our Lord used this expression, and it occurs in this same gospel near the beginning, where in the narrative of the first cleansing of the temple we read that He said, "Make not My Father's house a house of merchandise." The earlier use of the words may help to throw light upon one aspect of this latter employment of it, for there blend in the image the two ideas of what I may call domestic familiarity, and of that great future as being the reality of which the earthly temple was intended to be the dim prophecy and shadow. Its courts, its many chambers, its ample porches with room for thronging worshipers, represented in some poor way the wide sweep and space of that higher house; and the sense of Sonship, which drew the boy to His Father's house in the earliest hours of conscious childhood, speaks here.

Think for a moment of how sweet and familiar the conception of heaven as the Father's house makes it to us. There is something awful, even to the best and holiest souls, in the thought of even the glories beyond. The circumstances of death, which is its portal, our utter unacquaintance with all that lies behind the veil, the terrible silence and distance which falls upon our dearest ones as they are sucked into the cloud, all tend to make us feel that there is much that is solemn and awful even in the thought of eternal future blessedness. But how it is all softened when we say, "My Father's house." Most of us have long since left behind us the sweet security, the sense of the absence of all responsibility, the assurance of defense and provision, which used to be ours when we lived as children in a father's house here. But we may all look forward to the renewal, in far nobler form, of these early days, when the father's house meant the impregnable fortress where no evil could befall us, the abundant home where all wants were supplied, and where the most shy and timid child could feel at ease and secure. It is all coming again, brother, and amidst the august and unimaginable glories of that future the old feeling of being little children, nestling safe in the Father's house, will fill our quiet hearts once more.

And then consider how the conception of that future as the Father's house suggests answers to so many of our questions about the relationship of the inmates to one another. Are they to dwell isolated in their several mansions? Is that the way in which children in a home dwell with each other? Surely if He be the Father, and heaven be His house, the relation of the redeemed to one another must have in it more than all the sweet familiarity and unrestrained frankness which subsists in the families of earth. A solitary heaven would be but half a heaven, and would ill correspond with the hopes that inevitably spring from the representation of it as "my Father's house."

But consider further that this great and tender name for heaven has its deepest meaning in the conception of it as a spiritual state of which the essential elements are the loving manifestation and presence of God as Father, the perfect consciousness of sonship, the happy union of all the children in one great family, and the derivation of all their blessedness from their Elder Brother.

The earthly temple, to which there is some allusion in this great metaphor, was the place in which the divine glory was manifested to seeking souls, though in symbol, yet also in reality, and the representation of our text blends the two ideas of the free, frank intercourse of the home and of the magnificent revelations of the Holy of holies. Under either aspect of the phrase, whether we think of *my Father's house* as temple or as home, it sets before us, as the main blessedness and glory of heaven, the vision of the Father, the consciousness of sonship, and the complete union with Him. There are many subsidiary and more outward blessings and glories which shine dimly through the haze of metaphors and negations, by which alone a state of which we have no experience can be revealed to us; but these are secondary. The heaven of heaven is the possession of God the Father through the Son in the expanding spirits of His sons. The sovereign and filial position which Jesus Christ in His manhood occupies in that higher house, and which He shares with all those who by Him have received the adoption of sons, is the very heart and nerve of this great metaphor.

But I think we must go a step further than that, and recognize that in the image there is inherent the teaching that that glorious future is not merely a state, but also a place. Local associations are not to be divorced from the words; and although we can say but little about such a matter, yet everything in the teaching of Scripture points to the thought that howsoever true it may be that the essence of heaven is condition, yet that also heaven has a local habitation, and is a place in the great universe of God. Jesus Christ has at this moment a human body, glorified. That body, as Scripture teaches us, is somewhere, and where He is there shall also His servant be. In the context He goes on to tell us that He goes to prepare a place for us, and though I would not insist upon the literal interpretation of such words, yet distinctly the drift of the representation is in the direction of localizing, though not of materializing, the abode of the blessed. So I think we can say, not merely that *what* He is that shall also His servants be, but that *where* He is there shall also His servants be. And from the representation of my text, though we cannot fathom all its depths, we can at least grasp this, which gives solidity and reality to our contemplations of the future, that heaven is a place, full of all sweet security and homelike repose, where God is made known in every heart and to every consciousness as a loving Father, and of which all the inhabitants are knit together in the frankest fraternal intercourse, conscious of the Father's love, and rejoicing in the abundant provisions of His royal House.

There Is Room for All in the Father's House

And then there is a second thought to be suggested from these words, and that is of the ample room in this great house. The original purpose of the words of my text, as I have already reminded you, was simply to soothe the fears of a handful of disciples.

There was room where Christ went for eleven poor men. Yes, room enough for them! But Christ's prescient eye looked down the ages, and saw all the unborn millions that would yet be drawn to Him, and some glow of satisfaction flitted across His sorrow, as He saw from afar the result of the impending travail of His soul in the multitudes by whom God's heavenly house should yet be filled. *Many mansions*! the thought widens out far beyond our grasp. Perhaps that upper room, like most of the roof-chambers in Jewish houses, was open to the skies, and while He spoke, the innumerable lights that blaze in that clear heaven shone down upon them, and He may have pointed to these. The better Abraham perhaps looked forth, like His prototype, on the starry heavens, and saw in the vision of the future those who through Him should receive the "adoption of sons" and dwell forever in the house of the Lord, "so many as the stars of the sky in multitude, and as the sand which is by the seashore innumerable."

Ah! brethren, if we could only widen our measurement of the walls of the New Jerusalem to the measurement of that "golden rod which the man, that is the angel," as John says, applied to it, we should understand how much bigger it is than any of these poor sects and communities of ours here on earth. If we would lay to heart, as we ought to do, the deep mining of that indefinite *many* in my text, it would rebuke our narrowness. There will be a great many occupants of the mansions in heaven that Christian men here on earth will be very much surprised to see there, and thousands will find their entrance there that never found their entrance into any communities of so-called Christians here on earth.

That one word many should deepen our confidence in the triumphs of Christ's Cross, and it may be used to heighten our own confidence as to our own poor selves. A chamber in the great Temple waits for each of us, and the question is, Shall we occupy it, or shall we not? The old rabbis had a tradition which, like a great many of their apparently foolish sayings, covers in picturesque guise a very deep truth. They said that, however many the throngs of worshipers who came up to Jerusalem at the Passover, the streets of the city and the courts of the sanctuary were never crowded. And so it is with that greater city. There is room for all. There are throngs, but no crowds. Each finds a place in the ample sweep of the Father's house like some of the great palaces that barbaric Eastern kings used to build, in whose courts armies might encamp, and the chambers of which were counted by the thousand. And surely in all that ample accommodation, you and I may find some corner where we, if we will, may lodge forevermore.

I do not dwell upon subsidiary ideas that may be drawn from the expressions. *Mansions* means places of permanent abode, and suggests the two thoughts, so sweet to travelers and toilers in this fleeting, laboring life, of unchangeableness and of repose. Some have supposed that the variety in the attainments of the redeemed, which is reasonable and scriptural, might be deduced from our text, but that does not seem to be relevant to our Lord's purpose.

One other suggestion may be made without enlarging upon it. There is only one other occasion in this gospel in which the word here translated "mansions" is employed, and it is this: "We will come and make our abode with him." Our mansion is in God; God's dwelling place is in us. So ask yourselves, Have you a place in that heavenly home? When a prodigal child goes away from the father's house, sometimes a brokenhearted parent will keep the boy's room just as it used to be when he was young and pure, and will hope and weary through long days for him to come back and occupy it again. God is keeping a room for you in His house; do see that you fill it.

We Know as Much as We Need to Know

In the next place, note here the sufficiency of Christ's revelation for our needs.

"If it were not so I would have told you." He sets Himself forward in very august fashion as being the Revealer and Opener of that house for us. There is a singular tone about all our Lord's few references to the future—a tone of decisiveness; not as if He were speaking, as a man might do, that which he had thought out, or which had come to him, but as if He was speaking of what He had Himself beheld. "We speak that we do know, and testify that we have seen." He stood like One on a mountaintop, looking down into the valleys beyond, and telling His comrades in the plain behind Him what He saw. He spoke of that unseen world always as One who had been in it, and who was reporting experiences, and not giving forth opinions. His knowledge was the knowledge of One who dwelt with the Father, and left the house in order to find and bring back His wandering brethren. It was "His own calm home, His habitation from eternity," and therefore He could tell us with decisiveness, with simplicity, with assurance, all which we need to know about the geography of that unknown land—the plan of that, by us unvisited, house. Very remarkable, therefore, is it, that with this tone there should be such reticence in Christ's references to the future. The text implies the *rationale* of such reticence. "If it were not so I would have told you." I tell you all that you need, though I tell you a great deal less than you sometimes wish.

The gaps in our knowledge of the future, seeing that we have such a Revealer as we have in Christ, are remarkable. But my text suggests this to us—we have as much as we need. *I* know, and many of *you* know, by bitter experience, how many questions, the answers to which would seem to us to be such a lightening of our burdens, our desolated and troubled hearts suggest about that future, and how vainly we ply heaven with questions and interrogate the unreplying Oracle. But we know as much as we need. We know that God is there. We know that it is the Father's house. We know that Christ is in it. We know that the dwellers there are a family. We know that sweet security and ample provision are there; and, for the rest, if we needed to have heard more, He would have told us.

> My knowledge of that life is small,
> The eye of faith is dim;
> But 'tis enough that Christ knows all;
> And I shall be with Him.

Let the gaps remain. The gaps are part of the revelation, and we know enough for faith and hope.

May we not widen the application of that thought to other matters than to our bounded and fragmentary conceptions of a future life? In times like the present, of doubt and unrest, it is a great piece of Christian wisdom to recognize the limitations of our knowledge and the sufficiency of the fragments that we have. What do we get a revelation for? To solve theological puzzles and dogmatic difficulties? to inflate us with the pride of quasi-omniscience? or to present to us God in Christ for faith, for love, for obedience, for imitation? Surely the latter, and for such purposes we have enough.

So let us recognize that our knowledge is very partial. A great stretch of wall is blank, and there is not a window in it. If there had been need for one, it would have been struck out. He has been pleased to leave many things obscure, not arbitrarily, so as to try our faith—for the implication of the words before us is that the relation between Him and us binds Him to the utmost possible frankness, and that all which we need and He can tell us He does tell—but for high reasons, and because of the very conditions of our present environment, which forbid the more complete and all-round knowledge.

So let us recognize our limitations. We know in part, and we are wise if we affirm in part. Hold by the Central Light, which is Jesus Christ. "Many things did Jesus which are not written in this Book," and many gaps and deficiencies from a human point of view exist in the contexture of revelation. "But these are written that ye may believe that Jesus is the Christ," for which enough has been told us, "and that, believing, ye may have life in His name." If that purpose be accomplished in us, God will not have spoken, nor we have heard, in vain. Let us hold by the Central Light, and then the circumference of darkness will gradually retreat, and a wider sphere of illumination be ours, until the day when we enter our mansions in the Father's house, and then "in Thy Light shall we see light"; and we shall "know even as we are known."

Let your Elder Brother lead you back, dear friend, to the Father's bosom, and be sure that if you trust Him and listen to Him, you will know enough on earth to turn earth into a foretaste of heaven, and will find at last your place in the Father's house beside the Brother who has prepared it for you.

NOTES

A Glimpse of the Afterlife

Clovis Gillham Chappell (1882–1972) was one of American Methodism's best-known and most effective preachers. He pastored churches in Washington, DC; Dallas and Houston, Texas; Memphis, Tennessee; and Birmingham, Alabama; and his pulpit ministry drew great crowds. He was especially known for his biographical sermons that made biblical figures live and speak to our modern day. He published about thirty volumes of sermons.

This message was taken from *The Village Tragedy*, published in 1975 by Abingdon Press.

Clovis Gillham Chappell

8

A GLIMPSE OF THE AFTERLIFE

And in hell he lift up his eyes (Luke 16:23).

WHILE SO MUCH is being said about the afterlife, so much that is false, so much that is misleading and bewildering, it seems to me altogether wise to learn something of what is said by Him who speaks with authority. The story that I have read to you fell from the lips of Jesus Christ our Lord. It was uttered by Him "who came from God and who went to God." It is altogether wise to remember this. Philosophers, scholars, and wise men may speculate, and do speculate, about what lies beyond the grave. Our Lord does not speculate—He knows. He is equally at home in the realm of the seen and of the unseen. He is as familiar with the yonder as He is with the here and now.

For this reason we have a right to come to this story with confidence. We have a right to come to it with reverent expectation. It was uttered by Him who of old laid the foundations of the world, by Him who was in the beginning with God, and who is God. Its teachings are the teachings of Him in whom "dwelt all the fullness of the God-head bodily." If there is that in the story which seems to you absurd, remember that it is the utterance of eternal wisdom. If there is that in the story that seems to you heartless and cruel, bear in mind that it is the cruelty of Him who loved us well enough to hang on the nails for our redemption.

As I speak to you about this wonderful story, then, I shall speak with conviction. I shall feel no fear that the ground on which I stand will have a hollow ring as I tread upon it. For I have this confidence in my Lord—He is too wise to be mistaken and too honest to deceive us. When

He had the last conversation with His disciples on this side of the grave, He said to them, "Let not your heart be troubled. In my Father's house are many mansions. If it were not so I would have told you." That is, "I would not allow you to believe what is false, even though it was a comfortable belief. I would not allow you to rest your heads upon falsehood, even though it might be as soft as pillows of down. I tell you that there is a Homeland of the Soul. I say this, not because it meets the deepest yearnings of your hearts, but because it is true." So in the story that we have before us we may expect to find that about the afterlife which is true.

Look now at the story. It is really a wonderful drama in three scenes. The first scene reveals a typical day in the lives of two men.

Scene 1

"There was a certain rich man that was clothed in purple and fine linen, and fared sumptuously every day.

"And there was a beggar named Lazarus that was laid at his gate, full of sores,

"And desiring to be fed with the crumbs that fell from the rich man's table; moreover the dogs came and licked his sores."

This then, is the picture upon which the Master lifts the curtain. He makes us see these two individuals. He shows us how they live. He compels us to look at the rich man and also to look at the beggar. That is all. He utters no word of comment upon the character of either man.

Here is the scene: A lovely palace. You enter the palace through a magnificent portal. The halls are lined with "marble white and black, like the mingling of night and morning." The rooms are hung with the finest of tapestries. And the rugs upon the floor are the choicest product of the oriental loom. There are courts of rare beauty where fountains spray from silver faucets and make lovely and listless music.

Today there is a big banquet at the palace. The select Four Hundred are being entertained. The host receives graciously. He is the best dressed man of the company.

He is cultured, refined, elegant, rich. The guests whom he welcomes are likewise elegant and refined and rich.

The scene is altogether pleasing but for one thing. There is one blot upon its beauty. There is one ugly scar upon its loveliness. At the outer gate of this palatial home there lies a bundle of dirty rags. As we look we see the rags stir a bit. It is a sick beggar that is within them trying to make himself comfortable upon the cobblestones. He too seems to be receiving today. But his guests are not refined and cultured. They are the wild, unfriended dogs of the street. These sit about him on their haunches and lick his sores. They too are starved and friendless, but withal they seem less friendless than the sick man whom they are attending.

You will notice at once that Christ has no word of condemnation for the rich man because he is rich or because he feeds well or because he wears fine clothes. Nor is there any attempt on His part to put a halo upon the beggar's head because of his poverty and rags and sickness. He simply puts the scene before us. We are forced to look at these two men. Physically they are close together. In point of circumstance they are far apart. The one is sick; the other is well. The one is rich; the other is poor. The one fares sumptuously every day; the other feeds on crumbs. The one has friends and the other is unfriended. And as we look we realize that the tragedy of the picture is that the two never actually come together.

"There was a certain rich man"—what is the meaning of the word? Rich man—it stands for power, capacity, ability to serve. "And there was a beggar that lay at his gate full of sores"—that means need. And so we have here ability to serve and a need of service brought close together. The poor man was at the rich man's gate. That means that this poor man was the rich man's responsibility. He was the rich man's opportunity. I do not know what responsibility lay at the gate of the man across the street, but the responsibility of this rich man is very plain. The call for help is loud and insistent. Here was his chance. Here was his opportunity. Here was the safety vault in which he might have made a deposit for eternity.

But the rich man seems never to have seen the man at his gate. He was too busy with his affairs. He was too much occupied with his own pleasures, the pleasures of getting and the pleasures of spending. Not that he was unkind to the beggar—he did not have him stoned, he did not have him thrown into prison. He was not a cruel man, this rich man. At least, he was not aggressively cruel. I dare say he was better than the average. Otherwise he would have driven the old beggar away and not even allowed him to gather up the crumbs. At least the sin of the man was not that he did anything of harm to the beggar. It was rather in the fact that he let him alone.

Scene 2

The second scene is one familiar enough in our world. The rich man allowed the beggar to receive only the scraps, only the crumbs. Now, men cannot be saved by crumbs. God will never save the world through the mere crumbs of our time and of our energy and of our money. The beggar got only the crumbs, so quite naturally it came to pass that the beggar died.

"Ah," you say, "there is nothing startling about that." "I have been expecting him to die for a long time," one said. Another said, "He is out of his misery, better off. To have given him bread would have been a calamity as it might have caused him to suffer only the longer." Yes, the beggar died and nobody thought of being startled by it. Nobody thought of weeping over it. It was not at all disturbing even to the rich man, though if he had been faithful to his duty the beggar might have lived. Thousands die morally every year because we who are rich in resources, material and spiritual, are too self-centered to meet their needs.

"The rich man also died"—now, that is startling. We could easily spare the beggar, but a leading citizen that gave banquets—that is different. "The rich man also died"—he died in spite of his riches. He died in spite of his palace. He died in spite of his fine linen. One day ill mannered Death walked in with his boots muddy with the clay of new-made graves and pushed this self-centered, feasting man out into his tomb.

The rich man died and had a funeral. The funeral of the beggar is not mentioned. Doubtless he had none. His old sore body was found in the street and carted away with the day's garbage.

> Rattle his bones over the stones,
> He's only a beggar whom nobody owns.

But the rich man was buried. And here Christ drops the curtain.

Scene 3

When the curtain rises again it rises upon the world unseen.

"It came to pass that the beggar died and was carried by the angels into Abraham's bosom."

That is, he was carried into the Paradise of God.

"The rich man also died and was buried;

"And in Hades he lifted up his eyes, being in torment, and seeth Abraham afar off and Lazarus in his bosom."

How naturally Christ passes from the seen into the unseen. With what absolute at-homeness He shows us these two men as they are in the afterlife!

The Dead Are Still Alive

What are some of the facts that He tells us through this story? What light does He throw upon the mystery of the unseen? They are facts familiar enough to Bible readers. They have been pointed out many times before. First, He tells us very clearly and unmistakably that *the dead are still alive*, that the man who has passed into the unseen is not asleep. He is consciously and vividly alive. This is true of Lazarus; this is true also of Dives.

And this fact of the conscious, vivid life of those who have passed into the hereafter is not taught in this parable alone. Over and over again this same truth is either implied or clearly stated. In speaking of Abraham, Isaac, and Jacob, saints who had passed into the unseen, Jesus did not count them as dead. In fact, He clearly declared quite the contrary. "For

God," says He, "is not the God of the dead, but of the living."

When Jesus was hanging on the cross one of the men at His side prayed this marvelous prayer: "Lord, remember me when thou comest in thy Kingdom." And Jesus replied to that prayer by giving the dying robber this promise: "Today shalt thou be with me in Paradise." What did the promise mean? It means that Jesus and the dying robber were going to meet in the Paradise of God that very day; that they were going to be consciously alive and conscious of each other. So Death is not a sleep. All men are consciously alive beyond the grave.

The second fact we learn from this story is that these men are not only alive, but they are conscious of being themselves. Lazarus is still Lazarus. Dives is still Dives. The rich man still speaks of himself and says, "I." He is conscious of the fact that he is the same man on the further side of the grave that he was on this side. He is conscious of the same human relationships. He is conscious of the fact that he is the same individual who once knew Lazarus in this world, and who was also a member of a family of six brothers.

At death we are going to lose something, each of us. We are going to lose the physical. We are going to lose our possessions. Whatever may be our material wealth in this world, we may depend upon it that the hands of the dead are not clutching hands. Our shrouds will have no pockets. Death will rob us of all that is material.

But there is one something that Death cannot take away from us. It cannot rob us of ourselves. Yesterday I was myself. I will be myself still tomorrow. I will continue to be myself as long as heaven is heaven: as long as God is God.

Of course by saying that I will forever be myself I do not mean for a moment that I will forever possess this body that I possess tonight or this brain that I possess tonight. But this body is not myself. We are all aware of that. This body is a possession of mine. I own it. I control its movements. I can make it act in accordance with my will. I speak through its lips. I minister through its hands.

I look out from its open windows called eyes and receive messages through its open portals called ears. I own a body tonight. However, it is not the same body I once owned. I am fond of change. I get a new suit of clothes for this body now and then. I also get a new suit for this soul of mine at least once every seven years. So I have already worn out five bodies and thrown them away like a castoff garment. Yet I am still conscious of being the same self that I was the first body I ever owned.

And of course it is not saying anything new to say that my brain is not myself. I possess a brain, but this brain does not control me. I control it. I have power to educate it. I have power to direct its energy. I have power to focus its thinking upon a certain object. I am in the possession of a brain, but I do not possess the same brain I once had. Neither do you. We wear out brains just as we wear out bodies. It is really amazing how some of us wear our brains out using them as little as we do, but we wear them out nonetheless. And I have had at least five different sets of brains, and yet I am still the same individual that I was when I was in possession of the first brain I ever had.

Now, if I can throw away five different bodies and five different brains and still be the same man, I can throw away this body and brain into the grave at the end of the day and still be the same. The truth of the matter is, death is not going to touch me personally at all. It is not going to touch the real "me." For this reason I am going to be exactly the same man the first minute after death as I was the last minute before death. It would work no great moral change in me to pass from one side of the Potomac River to the other, nor would it work any great change for me to pass from one side of the narrow river called Death to the other.

In spite of this fact, however, there is a tremendously great tendency to believe that death will work a moral change, that you can lie down one moment self-centered, sin-conquered, godless—and by the mere act of dying, wake up the next moment holy, sinless and Christlike. It is absolutely false. If Christ does not save you in the here and now, do not expect death to accomplish what He was unable to accomplish. If the blood of Jesus Christ cannot cleanse you from all sin, do not be so mad as to expect that cleansing at the hands of the undertaker, the shroud, and the coffin. Believe me, that as death finds you, so you will be the instant after when you open your eyes in the world unseen.

The third fact Christ teaches us in this story is that man is not only alive and conscious of self beyond the grave, but that *he remembers*. Lazarus remembered Dives and Dives remembered Lazarus. They remembered their former experiences. Dives remembered the life he used to live. He remembered his selfishness and his sin. He remembered his lost opportunities. He remembered the five brothers in the home from whence he had come, and how his own life had helped them to be selfish and godless like himself. In the afterlife you are going to remember. Memory is going to be a power that will help to intensify the joys of heaven. It will also help to embitter the pangs of hell.

The Choice: Live for God or Live for Self

Finally, Christ makes it plain to us in this story that *all men are not going to have the same destiny* in the world unseen. He teaches us that there is going to be a separation there between the good and the bad, between the Christlike and the Christless. These two men in the world unseen were separated. Between them, we are told, there was a great gulf fixed. Who separated them? God, you say? I deny it. They separated themselves. The chasm between Dives and Lazarus was made in this life. They made different choices here. Those different choices led to different characters. They became morally separated by a chasm as wide as right from wrong, as night from day. And that separation continued beyond the grave.

Why was Lazarus carried by the angels into Abraham's bosom? It was not because in this life he was unfortunate. It was not because he was friendless and attended in his last illness only by dogs. It was not because he was sick and sore and neglected. He was carried into heaven because in spite of all these calamities, he made choice of

God. His name signifies, "God is my help." And it was this right choice that made him a right character. And this right character made for a glorious spiritual destiny.

Dives, on the other hand, was not lost simply because he was rich. He was not cast out because he wore fine clothes and had sumptuous feasts. Dives was ruined by a wrong choice. Listen to the story. He is asking for a drop of water to cool his parching tongue. And the reply he receives is this: "Remember that thou in thy lifetime receivedst thy good things, likewise Lazarus evil things."

What does it mean? This: "Remember that in your lifetime you made a deliberate choice of the things that are seen. You deliberately chose to live for self. You turned your back upon God, and turning your back upon God, you turned it upon your own brother. You chose to live for the gratification of your own pleasure." That is what brought ruin to Dives—not the fact that he was rich, not the fact that he lived well, but the fact that he deliberately chose to ignore God and to live for self.

Not only did Dives choose to live for himself, but he chose it in the face of the light. He knew better. He knew the life that he ought to live. When he is refused the drop of water, he asks that Lazarus be sent to his five brothers to warn them, thus implying that he was not rightly warned, that if he had had proper warning he himself would never have made the fatal choice that he did make and achieve the fatal destiny that he had achieved. But the reply to this is very emphatic and very clear. He is told, "Your brothers have Moses and the prophets. That is light enough. And if they will not hear them, if they will not be persuaded by them, neither will they be persuaded though one rose from the dead."

Men are accustomed to flatter themselves with the belief that they would change their lives and become Christians if certain positive proofs of the life to come were brought to them. But Christ tells us that men are not convinced by ghosts. Men are not led to repentance by ouija boards and seances. I have known quite a number who claim to have received messages from the dead. I have never known one single one who has been made a

New Testament type of Christian by such messages. God's only method of reaching men is through the truth believed in and obeyed, and if men will not hear that they will not be saved, even though one rises from the dead.

Thus it came to pass that Lazarus found himself in Abraham's bosom. It is a Hebrew way of saying that he was in the Paradise of God. He was in a place of comfort. He was in a place of joy. Dives, on the other hand, was in a place of conscious pain. While Lazarus was comforted Dives was tormented. Why was this true? It was not because God loved the one and did not love the other. It was not because God desired to save one and did not desire to save the other. Their different destinies were the inevitable outcome, I repeat, of their different characters, as their different characters were the outcome of their different choices.

The truth of the matter is that God has no way of getting any man into heaven when he has hell in his own heart. You cannot mix the living and the dead even in this life. A little child was last week carried out of a home where it was the idol, and buried. The reason for this conduct on the part of the father and mother was not because they no longer loved the child. They buried the child in spite of their love for it, because it was dead. And hell, whatever else it may be, is the burying ground of dead souls, souls that are dead in trespasses and in sin.

So the conclusion of the whole matter is this: Forever you are going to live. Forever you are going to be yourself. You are going to have to keep house with yourself for all eternity. Forever you are going to remember. Forever you are going to enjoy or suffer the destiny that you make for yourself while in this life. If it sounds foolish remember it is the foolishness of Him "who spake as never man spake." If it seems heartless, remember that it is the heartlessness of Infinite Love. Remember, too, that though some men are lost, no man needs to be lost. Every man can be saved if he will. This minute you can be saved if you will only be wise enough and brave enough to make a right choice. "Him that cometh unto me I will in no wise cast out." Will you come? Will you come now?

NOTES

The Barrier

Charles Haddon Spurgeon (1834–1892) is undoubtedly the most famous minister of the last century. Converted in 1850, he united with the Baptists and soon began to preach in various places. He became pastor of the Baptist church in Waterbeach in 1851, and three years later he was called to the decaying Park Street Church, London. Within a short time, the work began to prosper, a new church was built and dedicated in 1861, and Spurgeon became London's most popular preacher. In 1855, he began to publish his sermons weekly; today they make up the fifty-seven volumes of *The Metropolitan Tabernacle Pulpit*. He founded a pastor's college and several orphanages.

This sermon is taken from *The Metropolitan Tabernacle Pulpit*, Volume 27, and was preached on March 27, 1881.

Charles Haddon Spurgeon

9

THE BARRIER

And there shall in no wise enter into it any thing that defileth, neither whatsoever worketh abomination, or maketh a lie: but they which are written in the Lamb's Book of Life (Revelation 21:27).

THE TEXT REFERS to the glorified church of our Lord Jesus Christ. That perfected company of the elect and sanctified is set forth in this wonderful chapter under the image of a city descending "from God out of heaven, prepared as a bride adorned for her husband." Her workday dress all laid aside, the bride appears in garments of needlework and raiment of wrought gold. The militant church, the church of the present day, is comparable to a tent, and is well imaged by the tabernacle in the wilderness: it is lit up within by the glory of God's presence, and covered without by the fiery cloudy pillar of His eternal providence; but yet to the eyes of men it is mean and inconsiderable, for verily it does not yet appear what it shall be. By-and-by this same church, which today is likened unto a structure of curtains readily removed from place to place, shall become a city, fixed, permanent, high-walled, and compact together, a "city which hath foundations, whose builder and maker is God." The discomforts and trials of the desert life shall be exchanged for the quiet and comfort of a city dwelling. There shall be nothing of the wilderness about the church triumphant; it shall be a right royal abode, the metropolis of the universe, the palace of the great King. Everything that is lustrous, pure, precious, majestic shall be there. Rare and priceless things which are now the peculiar treasure of kings shall be the common possession of all the sanctified. The church shall be no longer despised, but shall sit as a queen among the nations, while at her feet they shall heap up all their glory and honor. In that church there shall remain nothing for which men shall reproach her, but everything shall be manifested in her for which they shall do her honor; her very streets to be trodden on shall be of pure gold like unto transparent glass, and her lowest course of stones shall be of jasper. Everything about the perfected church shall be the best of the best: she shall be recognized as being the fairest among women, the bride, the Lamb's wife, the crown and flower of the universe. We read the sparkling figures of John's vision as emblems of moral and spiritual excellence, but we doubt not that, beyond the spiritual riches of the church, all materialism will also be at her disposal, and the restored creation shall bring her choicest beauties to adorn the chosen bride of the Lamb.

Crown of the New Creation

We have said that the glorified church will be the crown of the new creation, and it is into the new heavens and the new earth that she is represented as coming down from God. He that sits upon the throne said "Behold, I make all things new." The creation which is round about us at this hour waxes old, and is ready to vanish away. Wise men tell us that there are evident preparations in the bowels of the earth for a burning up of the earth and of all the works of men that are upon it, for its center is an ocean of fire. God shall but speak, and as once the waters leaped upon the world and utterly destroyed all things that were upon it, so shall He call to the waves of flame and they shall rise from their hidden furnaces to melt all things with their fervent heat. Nevertheless we, according to His promise, look for new heavens and a new earth, wherein dwells righteousness. The former things shall have passed away, and a new creation shall dwell beneath the new heavens, filling up the new earth; and the flower and perfection of the new creation shall be the church of the living God in her full bloom and perfectness. Even now the regenerate are a kind of first fruits of God's creatures, the forerunners of the renewed universe; but then they shall be its center and glory. The new birth is the beginning of the new creation: we lead the way, even we who are the church of the firstborn, but the whole creation groans to follow us so as to be delivered from the bondage of corruption into the glorious liberty of the children of God.

It is the glorified church, I say, that is here spoken of, and hence the text may be said to refer to heaven, for at the present moment the nucleus of the glorified church is in heaven, and from heaven every defiled thing must be shut out. Hence, too, it may refer to the kingdom of the millennial age, when the saints will reign with Christ upon the earth for a thousand years, when even upon this battlefield our conquering Leader shall be crowned with victory, and where His blood was shed His throne shall be set up, for among the sons of men shall He triumph, even among those that spat in His face. The text may also be read as including the eternal world of future bliss, for of that glorious, endless, undefiled inheritance the church glorified will be the possessor, but out of her shall long before have been gathered all things that offend, and them that do iniquity. From heaven and from all heavenly joys and states sin must be shut out. Into the perfected church there shall never enter anything that defiles, and from all its honors and rewards every polluted person is shut out by immutable decree.

The Glory of God

I should like you for a minute or two to think of that perfected church as she is described in this chapter, for it is a description worthy of the most profound study. What glory will surround the risen saints in their capacity as the city of God: "having the glory of God," says the eleventh verse. What a glory of glories is this! Even now, my brethren and sisters, you that are in Christ possess the grace of God, but you shall by-and-by conspicuously shine with the glory of God. At present you share in the dishonor which falls to the lot of your Master and His cause among a wicked generation, but then you shall share in the glory which is the reward of the travail of His soul. "Then shall the righteous shine forth as the sun in the kingdom of their Father." How glorious will that church be whose light shall be the presence of God Himself—light in which the nations of them that are saved shall rejoice. O my

God, write my name among them! And to that end write me among Your persecuted saints below. Well may we be content to endure what little of shame shall come upon the church militant on earth if we may participate in the honor of the church glorified above, for this is a glory which excels, "having the glory of God."

Massive and Vast

The city is described as exhibiting great massiveness, for the length and the breadth and the height of it are equal. It is a solid square, perfect and compact:

> Thy walls are made of precious stones,
> Thy bulwarks diamond square.

What a church will the church of God be in those happier days! Now she is as a rolling thing, removed as readily as a shepherd's tent; but then she shall stand firm as a cube which rests upon its base. We watch the church of God sometimes with trepidation and alarm, for though we know that the gates of hell shall not prevail against her, yet her feebleness makes the timid tremble; but in her state after the resurrection there shall remain no signs of feebleness, for that which was sown in weakness shall be raised in power. She shall be a city the like of which has never been beheld, whose foundation shall be deeper than the depths beneath, and her towers shall reach above the clouds. No institution shall exist so long or flourish so abundantly as the church of the living God.

When you think of the massiveness of the church of God, settled in her place by the Almighty Himself who has established her, remember at the same time her vastness, for a multitude that no man can number shall be comprehended among her inhabitants: her census shall prove her citizens to be as the stars of heaven for multitude. Her stones shall not lie cast about as a little heap, but from her vast foundation the living stones shall rise course upon course, twelve foundations of jewels till "the mountain of the Lord's house shall be exalted above the hills." I say again, write my name down among the dwellers in the great city! What higher honor can I crave than to have it said, "this man was born there"? To be numbered with princes, to be named with emperors, what of it! Your golden fleece, and silken garter, and gilded star are all poor toys; true glory lies in being part and parcel of the church, today despised and rejected of men, which shall ere long look forth fair as the sun, and astonish the world with the brightness of her rising. Ambition's self needs ask no more than citizenship in the heavenly Jerusalem.

Joys and Treasures and Pleasures and Delights

The perfection of the church is set forth in her being foursquare, her value in the sight of God by her walls being composed of the rarest gems, and her delights in the variety of the sparkling jewels which bedeck her, there being scarcely one precious stone omitted of those that were known to Orientals, while some are mentioned which are scarcely known to us at all. All manner of joys and treasures and pleasures and delights, every form and shade of excellence, virtue, and bliss shall belong to the perfected ones when their number and character shall be complete, and they shall be comparable to the city of God.

The safety and quiet of the church is set forth by her gates forever open. In times of war the city gates are fast closed, but for the New Jerusalem there will remain no fear of foe, no need to set a watch against an invader. Gog and Magog will be slain, and Armageddon's battle fought and finished, and unbroken rest shall be the portion of the glorified. Write my name among them, O my God, and permit me to enter into Your rest.

Best of all, remark how holy will the church be. She shall have no temple within her walls, for this simple reason, that she shall be all temple; she shall have no spot reserved for sacred uses, because all shall be "holiness unto the Lord." The divine presence shall be in all and over all, and this shall be the joy of her joy, "The glory of God did lighten it, and the Lamb is the light thereof." Brethren, the glory of the church even here below is the presence of God in her midst, but what will that presence be when it shines forth in noonday brightness? when spirits strengthened for the vision shall endure with transport the full splendor of

Jehovah's throne? Tongue cannot tell the glory, for thought cannot conceive it. Write my name among the blessed who shall see Jehovah's face. O living God, my soul thirsts after You. To dwell in Your presence is the summit of the soul's delight; to be with You where You are, and to behold Your glory, is the heaven of heaven. To what beyond this can thoughts aspire?

The Word of Exclusion

It being declared that the glorified church is to be all this, and a great deal more, of which we cannot now speak particularly, we may well long to enter within her gates of pearl. But what does the text say? I beseech you listen attentively to the solemn sound of THE WORD OF EXCLUSION— *"There shall in no wise enter into it anything that defileth, neither whatever worketh abomination, or maketh a lie."* Listen, I say, to this word of exclusion, though it sounds like a death-knell in my ears. Learn that it can be abundantly justified to the conscience of all thoughtful men; learn that your own soul, if it be honest, must set its seal to the sentence of exclusion. This is no arbitrary decree, it is a solemn declaration to which all holy spirits give their willing assent and consent; an ordinance of which even the excluded themselves shall admit the justice.

For, first, *it is not meet that so royal and divine a corporation as the glorified church of God should be ruined by defilement.* God forbid that "her light, which is like unto a stone most precious, even like a jasper stone, clear as crystal," should ever be dimmed by the breath of sin. How beautiful was this fair world in the early morning of her creation, when the dew of her youth glistened upon her, and the sunlight of God made her face to shine. Keep watch and ward, you shining ones, that this beauty be not marred! Let watchers and holy ones fly around the new-made world to drive far hence the apostate spirit and his fellows who kept not their first estate. Sad was the hour when with dragon wing the fallen spirit descended into Eden, advanced to mother Eve, and whispered in her ear the fell temptation. Oh, seraphs, would God your fiery swords had kept out the arch-deceiver, that this world might never have fallen, that we might have dwelt here amidst sunny glades, by pure rivers rippling over sands of gold, a holy and happy race, making every hill and vale vocal with the praise of God. Now, O earth, you are a field of blood, but you might have been a garden of delights; now are you one vast cemetery, where all the dust was once a part of the living fabric of mortal men, but you might have been as the firmament filled with stars, all shining to their Creator's praise. Alas that Eden should now remain only as a name—gone as a vision of the night!

Inasmuch as we could heartily wish that evil had never entered into the primeval world, we earnestly deprecate the idea that it should ever defile the new. Shall those new heavens ever look down with amazement upon the flight of a rebellious spirit, flying, beneath their serene azure, on an errand of destruction? Shall the jeweled walls of the thrice holy city be over-leaped by an enemy of the King who is there enthroned? Shall the serpent leave his horrid trail upon the heavenly Eden, twice made of the Lord? God forbid! The purity of a world twice made, the perfection of the church of the regenerate, the majesty of the presence of God, all demand that every sinful thing should be excluded. All heaven and heavenly things cry, "Write the decree and make it sure, there shall in no wise enter into it anything that defileth." Grave it as in eternal brass, and let omnipotence go with the decree to execute it with the utmost rigor, for it would be horrible indeed if a second time evil should destroy the work of God. Into the church of the first-born above the breath of iniquity must not enter. It cannot be that the work which cost the Redeemer's blood should yet be defiled. The eternal purpose of the Father, and the love of the Spirit, forbid that the Lord's own perfected church should be invaded by any unholy thing.

Brethren, there can be no entrance of evil into the kingdom of God, for *it is the very essence of the bliss of the glorified church that evil should be excluded*. Imagine for a moment that the decree of our text were reversed or suspended, and that it were allowed that a few unregenerate men and women should enter into the glorified church of God. Suppose, in addition, that those few should be of the gentler sort of sinners, not those who would profanely blaspheme the name of God, nor openly break the eternal Sabbath, but a few who are indifferent to God's glory, and cold and formal in His praise. How could heaven bear with these? These who are neither cold nor hot are sickening both to Christ and to His people, and must they endure the nausea of their society? Why, as in a living body the existence of a dead piece of bone breeds fret, and pain, and disease, so would the presence of these few defiling ones cause I know not what of disquietude and sorrow. It must not be.

Love to the saints demands that they be no more vexed by sin or sinners. Pity, mercy, yea, even the partiality of kindred love dare not ask that it may be. All heaven is up in arms at the supposition. Holy spirits are alarmed at the idea that they should be again tempted by the presence of evil. Fast bar the gates of pearl and never open them again, you spirits, rather than that there should come upon that pure street of transparent gold a foot that will not walk in the ways of God's commandments, or the halls of Zion be disgraced by a single spirit that shall refuse to love the holy and exalted name. Heaven were not heaven if it were possible for evil of any sort to enter there. Therefore, stand firm, O dread decree, for it would be cruelty to saints and destruction to heaven that there should in anywise enter into it anything that defiles.

Furthermore, let me beg you to consider that there is an impossibility of any defiled, sinful, unrenewed person ever entering into the body corporate of the glorified church of God—*an impossibility within the persons themselves.* Look, good sirs, the reason why wicked men cannot be happy is not alone because God will not let rebellion and peace dwell together, but because they will not let themselves be happy. The sea cannot rest because it is the sea, and the sinner cannot be quiet because he is a sinner. How could you, O natural, unregenerate man, ever enter into the kingdom of heaven as you are? You are not capable of it; it is not possible to you. Holiness has in it no attractions for you, since you love sin and the wages of it. You do not know God, and cannot see Him; for this is the privilege of the pure in heart, and of them alone. You live in a world where everything has been made by the great Lord, and yet you do not perceive His hand, so great is your blindness. Shall blind men grope through the streets of the New Jerusalem? You are unacquainted with the simplest elements of spiritual things; for they can only be spiritually discerned, and you have no spiritual faculty. You are blind and deaf, yes, dead to God and heavenly things—you know you are.

Well, then, of what avail would it be that you should enter the spiritual realm, supposing it to be a place? For if you were admitted into the place called heaven, you would not be a partaker of the state of heaven, and it is the state of mind and character which is, after all, the essence of the joy. To be in a heavenly place and not in a heavenly condition would be worse than hell, if worse can be. What are songs to a sad heart? Such would heaven be to an unrenewed mind. The element of glory would destroy rather than bless an unrenewed mind. It is as though you saw before you a blazing furnace, in which happy creatures disported themselves among the flames, bathing themselves in the white heat, leaping in rapture amid the rising sparks; for they are children of the flame, who drink in fire, and find it life.

Imagine yourself to be a poor fly such as you hear buzzing on the windowpane; and you ask to enter into the glow of the furnace, thinking to be as merry as the fire-children. Keep back. Why tempt your doom? You will die soon enough; why ask to perish more quickly? No place would be so dreadful to a sinner as the place where God is most openly manifest. That holy element, which is the habitat of the new-born soul, would be the grave, the everlasting prison-house of an unholy soul could it enter there. To the wicked the day of the Lord is darkness, and not light, and the glory of the Lord is terror, and not bliss.

Oh, unconverted hearer, they sing in heaven; but in their songs your ear would find no delight. They worship God in heaven; but as divine worship is irksome to you, even if it be kept up for an hour or so below, what would it be to dwell forever and ever in the world to come in the midst of hallelujahs? O soul defiled with sin, you are incapable of heaven. The Roman Emperor Caligula, in his madness, made his horse first-consul of Rome; but his horse could not be a magistrate; it could not judge or govern, whatever the emperor might decree; though he fed it upon gilded oats from an ivory manger, it was a horse and nothing more. Even so, if a man be unregenerate, and unbelieving, we may do what we will with him, but he cannot rise to spiritual joys, and if we could even bid him come into heaven, still he would remain what he was, incapable of the joy and bliss which God has prepared for them that love Him. So stands it a fact in the very essence and nature of things that there shall in no wise enter into the realm of the spiritual, the kingdom of the true, the land of the blessed, the home of the perfected, anything that defiles. It cannot come there from incapacity within itself.

Let me add that *our own hearts forbid that evil should so enter*. As I mused on this text I supposed myself to be defiled with sin, yet standing outside the pearl gates of heaven. Then I said within myself, "If I might enter there defiled as I am, would I do so?" and my heart answered, "No. I would not if I might. How could I blot such brightness and spoil such happiness?" Suppose myself infected today with a deadly fever—an incurable typhus, which would bring death to all that touched me. The blast is pitiless, and the snow is falling, and I stand shivering at the door of one of your houses longing for shelter. I see inside the room your little children, sporting in full health: shall I venture among them? I long to escape from the cold without; but if I should enter your room I should bring to you fever, and death to your innocent little ones and to yourselves, and thus turn your happiness into misery. I would turn away and brave the storm, and sooner die than bring such desolation into a friend's abode.

And well might any honest spirit say at sight of the perfect family above, "Nay, if I might, I would not be admitted into a perfect heaven while yet I might defile it, and spread the fell contagion of moral evil." You know, brethren, how a few rags from the East have sometimes carried a plague into a city; and if you were standing at the quay when a plague-laden ship arrived you would cry, "Burn those rags; do anything with them, but do keep them away from the people. Bring not the pest into a vast city, where it may slay its thousands!" So do we cry, "Great God, forbid it that anything that defiles should enter into Your perfected church! We cannot endure the thought thereof." Draw your swords, angels; stand in your serried ranks, seraphim, and smite every defiled one that would force a passage within the gates of pearl. It must be so: "There shall in no wise enter into it anything that defileth."

The fiat of God has gone forth, and the fiery sword is set at the gate of the new Eden. Into the first paradise there came the serpent; into the second never shall the subtle tempter enter. Into the first paradise there came sin, and God was driven from it as well as man; but into the second there shall never come anything that approximates to sin or falsehood; but the Lord God shall dwell there forever, and His people shall dwell there with Him. Thus much, then, upon the word of exclusion.

The Word of Exclusion Working Within the Soul

I desire, as I continue this meditation, in the power of the Holy Spirit, not so much to preach as to think inwardly, and ask you to think with me, of THAT WORD OF EXCLUSION WORKING WITHIN THE SOUL—within my soul, within yours. It sits in judgment upon me, and it chastens me. It strikes home to my conscience, and rouses me to self-examination. Its voice is solemn, and strikes heavily upon the ear, as we remember its wide sweep and comprehensive breadth—"There shall in no wise enter into it *anything* that defileth." No person who defiles, no fallen spirit, or sinful man can enter. And as no person, so no tendency, leaning, inclination, or will to sin can gain admission. No wish, no desire, no hunger toward that which is unclean shall ever be found in the perfect city of God. Nor even a thought of evil can be conceived there, much less a sinful act performed. Nothing shall ever be done within those gates of pearl contrary to the perfect law, nor anything imagined in opposition to spotless holiness.

Consider such purity, and wonder at it: the term *anything that defileth* includes even an idea, a memory, a thought of evil. Thoughts that flit through the mind as birds through the air that never roost or build a nest— even such shall never glance across the skies of the new creation. It is altogether perfect! And, mark well, that no untruth can enter—"neither whatsoever maketh a lie." Nothing can enter heaven which is not real; nothing erroneous, mistaken, conceited, hollow, professional, pretentious, unsubstantial, can be smuggled through the gates. Only truth can dwell with the God of truth. These are sweeping and searching words—no evil, nothing that works to evil; no falsehood, nothing that works to falsehood, can ever enter into the triumphant church of God. O my soul, my soul, how bears this upon you? Cuts it not to the very quick? For how are you to enter, defiled as you are, and so diseased with falsehood of one sort or another?

Well may we be aroused when we remember what defiled and defiling creatures we have been in the days of our unregeneracy. Brethren, let us not shrink from the humbling contemplation. Come down from your high places and see the horrible pit in which you lie by nature. Think of your past lives, I pray, of those days in which you found pleasure in walking after the flesh. I call on you to remember the sins of your youth, and your former transgressions, of thought, word, and deed. If they are shut out who defile, and are defiled, where are you? where are you? For these sins of ours, though they were committed years ago, are nonetheless sinful today; they are as fresh to God as if we perpetrated them this very moment.

You are still red-handed, O sinful man, though your crime was worked some twenty years ago. You are black, O sinner, still, though it be fifty years ago that your chief sin was committed; for time has no bleaching power upon a crimson sin. The guilt of an old offense is as fresh as though it were wrought but yesterday. Our sins in themselves make us unclean and unfit for holy company, and, alas, they are many. Our sins have left a second defilement on us, by creating the tendency to do the like again. Is there one among us that has sinned who does not know that he is all the more likely to sin again? Since after once being drawn aside by sin there are stronger draggings in the same way, sin once committed becomes a fountain of defilement. The stream in which the fish has sported will be sought by it again in its season, and the swallow will return to its old nest; even so will the mind return to its folly. Ay, so it is; and if everything that defiles is shut out from the holy city, my God, my God, am not I shut out too?

Bethink you that not only does actual sin shut men out of heaven, but this text goes to the heart by reminding us that we have within us inbred sin, which would defile us speedily, even if we were now clean of positive transgression. The fount from which actual sin comes is within every unrenewed bosom. How can you and I enter heaven while there is unholy anger in us? The best of men are too apt to retain an unhallowed quickness of temper, which, under certain circumstances works wrath. There shall in no wise enter into heaven a hasty temper, or a quick imperious spirit, or a malicious mind; for these defile. In certain persons there is no quickness of spirit, but there is a cold, chill obstinacy; so that having once resolved, though the resolve be evil, they stand to it doggedly and cannot be moved. Like obstinate mules, they can scarcely be driven; blows cannot stir them from their purpose. Disobedient obstinacy cannot enter the kingdom: my hearers, are you under its dominion?

And, oh, there is in all of us a lusting after evil of some sort or other. Only place us in certain conditions, and the flesh longs after forbidden things, and though we chide ourselves and check the longing, yet is there not within us a relish for the sweet stolen morsels of transgression? We could weep our eyes out when we discover what a palate for pleasurable sin our old nature still retains; yea, a longing for the very sin of which we most bitterly repent and from which we most eagerly long to be delivered. How can we hope to enter heaven if there be these appetites in us? They are there, and they defile! What can we do? There, too, is that vile thing called "pride." Why, some of us cannot be trusted with a pennyworth of success, but we are exalted above measure. Some of God's children cannot have ten minutes' fellowship with Christ but they must needs put on their fine feathers and crow right lustily because they feel themselves to be nearing absolute perfection. Alas for the pride of our hearts, and the pollution which comes of it! How can such vain creatures be admitted among the glorified?

Nor is this all; for sloth preys on many, and tempts them to shun God's service, and especially to shun the cross of Christ. Sloth is a rust which has a sadly defiling power: we gather moth and mildew from inaction. Never is a man pure who is not zealous in the service of God. We rot to corruption if we lie still; how, then, shall we be admitted within the jeweled city? Ah, look within your heart, my brother—look steadily beneath the fair film of the surface, and mark the inward evil which it conceals. Judge not yourself alone when at your best, occupied with your prayers and praises and almsgivings, but look steadily into your soul at other times, and you shall see a loathsome mass of evil life, a seething corruption moving within your heart; for evil remains even in the regenerate; and this cannot enter heaven. Thank God, it cannot. Even though the word of exclusion staggers me, and sends me back as with a stunning blow, and makes me cry, "Thou shuttest me out, my God, by this thy decree"; yet I feel that if it be so, the decree is right, and just, and good. "There shall in no wise enter into it anything that defileth." Amen and amen.

Now, I ask you whether this word of exclusion does not, in you who know its meaning, slay all hope of self-salvation? For, first, here are our past sins, and they defile, and make us defiling. How are we to get rid of them? How can we wash out these polluting blots? Tears! So much salt water thrown away if looked upon as a bath for sin! Good works performed! They are already due to God. How shall future discharge of debts repay the past? O my God, if I have ever known what sin means, I have also known that it is impossible that its defiling nature should ever be changed, or that the pollution should ever be removed by any efforts of my own.

I spoke with one the other day who said that she was

seeking salvation by good works. I knew that she had performed self-denying acts of charity, and I asked her whether she felt nearer to the salvation at which she aimed. I knew that I spoke to a sincere, honest person, and her reply did not surprise me. She answered sadly, "The more I do, the more I feel I ought to do, and I am no nearer to the point I am aiming at." And so it is; the more a sincere heart does seek to serve God, the more it feels the shortcoming of its service of Him; and the more a person seeks after purity by his own efforts, the further he judges himself to be from it. Our standard rises as we rise toward it; our conscience becomes tender in proportion as we obey it; and so, in the nature of things, rest of heart comes not in that manner. Ah, there remains not beneath heaven anything that can wash out the defilement of past sin save one only cleansing flood. O sinful man, plunge your hands into the Atlantic and you shall crimson every drop of its tremendous waters, and yet the stain shall be as scarlet as before. No, no, no: it is certain that no man can enter heaven, by reason of his transgression and his sinfulness, except omnipotence shall cleanse him.

But then look at the other part of the difficulty, that is, the making of your own heart pure and clean. How shall this be done? How shall the Ethiopian change his skin and the leopard his spots? Have you tried to master your temper? I hope you have. Have you managed it? Your tendencies this way or that, you have striven against them, I hope, but have you mastered them? I will tell you. You thought you had. You thought you had bound the enemy with strong ropes: you tied him and you fastened him down, and you shut him up in an inner chamber, and you said, "The Philistines be upon thee, Samson." You felt that the champion was vanquished now, but oh, how grimly did he laugh at you as the old adversary arose within you, and snapped the bonds, and hurled you to the ground; defeated when you thought that you had won the victory. I cannot overcome myself, nor overcome my sin. I will never cease from the task, God helping me, but apart from the divine Spirit the task is as impossible as to make a world.

The Word of Salvation

It seems to me that we may most fitly come to the close of our sermon by thinking of THE WORD OF SALVATION, which just meets the difficulty raised by the sentence: "There shall in no wise enter into it anything that defileth." But, first, my past sin, what of that? There are many who are even now within the church of God above, and we will ask concerning them, "Who are these arrayed in white robes, and whence came they?" We receive the reply, "These are they that have washed their robes, and made them white in the blood of the Lamb." "In the blood of the Lamb!"

I feel as if I could sing those words. What joy that there should be anything that can take all my stains away—all, without exception, and make me whiter than snow. If Christ be God, if it be true that He did within that infant's body contain the fullness of the Deity, and if, being thus God and man, He did take away my sin, and in His own body on the tree did bear it, and suffer its punishment for me, then I can understand how my transgression is forgiven and my sin is covered. Short of this my conscience cannot rest. The misty atonements of modern divines cannot calm my conscience; they are not worth the time spent in listening to them, they are cobwebs of the fancy, altogether insufficient to sustain the strain even of the present conscience, much less of the conscience which shall be aroused by the judgment bar of God. But this truth—Christ instead of me, God Himself the offended one in the offender's place, bowing His august head to vengeance and laying His eternal majesty in the dishonor of a tomb: this is the fullness of consolation.

O Lamb of God, my sacrifice, I shall enter heaven now! I shall pass the scrutiny of the infallible watchers. I shall not be afraid of the eyes of fire. I shall be without spot or wrinkle, or any such thing—"Washed in the blood of the Lamb!" This is our first great comfort, brethren—"He that believeth in him is not condemned." He that believes in Him is justified from all things from which he could not be justified by the law of Moses. "There is therefore now no condemnation to them that are in Christ Jesus."

But here is the point, there is still no entrance into the holy city so long as there are any evil tendencies within us. This is the work, this is the difficulty, and since these are to be overcome, how is the work to be done? Simple believing upon Christ brings you justification, but you want more than that; you need sanctification, the purgation of your nature, for have we not seen that until your nature itself is purged the enjoyment of heaven must be impossible? There can be no knowledge of God, no communion with God, no delight in God hereafter unless all sin is put away and your fallen nature is entirely changed.

Can this be done? It can. Faith in Christ tells us of something else beside the blood. There is a Divine Person—let us bow our heads and worship Him—the Holy Spirit who proceeds from the Father, and He it is who renews us in the spirit of our minds. When one believes in Jesus, the Spirit enters into the heart, creating within it a new life; that life struggles and contends against the old life, or rather the old death, and as it struggles it gathers strength and grows; it masters the evil, and puts its foot upon the neck of the tendency to sin. Do you feel this Spirit within you? You must be under its power or perish. If any man have not the Spirit of Christ he is none of His. I would not have you imagine that in death everything is to be accomplished for us mysteriously in the last solemn article; we are to look for a work of grace in life, a present work, molding our characters among men.

Oh, sirs, the sanctifying work of the Holy Spirit is not a sort of extreme unction reserved for deathbeds, it is a matter for the walks of life and the activities of today. I do not know how much is done in the saint during the last minute of his lingering here; but this I know, that in a true believer the conquest of sin is a matter to be begun as soon as he is converted and to be carried on throughout life. If the Spirit of God dwells in us, we walk not after the flesh but after the Spirit, and we mortify the corruptions and lusts of the old man. There must be now a treading under foot of lust and pride, and every evil thing, or these evils will tread us under foot forever in the future state where character never changes. There must be *now* a rejection of the lie, a casting out of the false, or we shall be cast out ourselves forever. There must be *now* a cry, "O Lord, thou desirest truth in the inward parts: and in the hidden part thou shalt make me to know wisdom. Purge me with hyssop, and I shall be clean: wash me, and I shall be whiter than snow." Beloved, it is to this we must come, to be washed in the water which flowed with the blood from Jesus' side, for there must be a purging of nature as well as a removal of actual transgression, or else the inevitable decree, like a fiery sword, will keep the gate of paradise against us. "There shall in no wise enter into it anything that defileth, neither whatsoever worketh abomination, or maketh a lie."

O my hearers, suppose we should never enter there! Nay, start not, for the supposition will soon be a fact with many of you except you repent. Suppose we should be in the next world what some of us are now, defiled and untruthful—what remains? That is an awful text in the parable of the virgins—"And the door was shut." You read of those who said, "Lord, Lord, open to us," to whom He answered, "I know you not." You have read of them, will anyone of us be among them? Will anyone of us who has a lamp, and is thought to be a virgin soul, be among the shut out ones, on whose ear shall fall the words, "I know you not whence you are."

You see you cannot be anywhere else but *out* unless you are in; and you must be shut out if you are defiled and defiling. Dear heart, this is a question I beg you to look to at once. You do not know how short a time you have left to you in which you may look into it. Some who were here but a Sabbath day or so ago are now gone from us. Eleven deaths reported at one church meeting among our members! We are a dying people; we shall all be gone within a very short time. I charge you by the living God, and as you are dying men and women, see to it that you are not shut out, so as to hear the fatal cry, "Too late, too late, you cannot enter now." There shall be no purgation in eternity, and no possible way of entering in among the perfected, for it is written, "There shall in no wise enter into it anything that defileth." No crying, "Lord! Lord!" no striving to enter in, no tears, no, not even the pangs of hell itself, shall ever purge the soul so as to make it fit to join with the holy church above, should it pass into the future state uncleansed. Shut out! shut out! O God, may that never be true of anyone among us, for Christ's dear name's sake. Amen.

Future Punishment Eternal

Robert Murray McCheyne (1813–1843) was one of the brightest lights of the Church of Scotland. Born in Dundee, he was educated in Edinburgh and licensed to preach in 1835. For a brief time, he assisted his friend, Andrew A. Bonar, at Larbert and Dunipace. In 1836 he was ordained and installed as pastor of St. Peter's Church, Dundee, where he served until his untimely death two months short of his thirtieth birthday. He was known for his personal sanctity and his penetrating ministry of the Word, and great crowds came to hear him preach. *The Memoirs of and Remains of Robert Murray McCheyne* by Andrew Bonar is a Christian classic that every minister of the gospel should read.

This sermon, preached July 15, 1842, is taken from *A Basket of Fragments*, published in Aberdeen by James Murray.

Robert Murray McCheyne

10

FUTURE PUNISHMENT ETERNAL

Where their worm dieth not, and the fire is not quenched (Mark 9:44).

IT IS VERY interesting to notice who they are in the Bible that speak about hell. Now, some think that speaking about hell is not preaching the gospel; and others think that simple men have no right to speak of it. Now, to them who think it is not gospel preaching, I say it is the truth—the Word of God; and to them who say it is not right to speak about it, I would have them to notice who it is that speaks most about it. Let us consider,

1. The persons in the Bible who speak most about hell.
2. Why these persons speak so plainly of hell.
3. The names given to hell.
4. The hell spoken of in the Bible is not annihilation.
5. This eternal hell is closed in and surrounded by the attributes of God.

1. The Persons in the Bible Who Speak About Hell

Let us consider the persons in the Bible who speak about hell. And the first I would mention is *David*. He was a man after God's own heart, yet he speaks of hell. He who wrote all the Psalms, the sweet Psalmist of Israel; he who was filled with love to men, and love to God; yet hear what he says about hell: "The sorrows of hell compassed me about" (Ps. 18:5). Again, "The sorrows of death compassed me about, and the pains of hell gat hold upon me" (Ps. 116:3). And hear of his deliverance: "And thou hast delivered my soul from the lowest hell" (Ps. 86:13). And he tells us also of the fate of the ungodly that will not accept Christ: "The wicked shall be turned into hell, and all the nations that forget God" (Ps. 9:17). "Upon the wicked he shall rain snares, fire, and brimstone, and an horrible tempest; this shall be the portion of their cup" (Ps. 11:6). "Let death seize upon them, and let them go down quick into hell" (Ps. 55:15). Now, whatever you think of the propriety of speaking about hell, David did not think it wrong, for he sang about it.

The next person I would mention is *Paul*. He was filled with the love of Christ, and he had great love to sinners. Surely that love wherewith God loved Jesus was in Paul. He loved his enemies: notice when he stood before Agrippa, what his feelings were, "I would to God that not only thou, but also all that hear me this day, were both almost and altogether such as I am, except these bonds" (Acts 26:29). He wished them to have the same love—the same joy—the same peace—the same hope of glory. Now, Paul never mentions the word *hell*. It seemed as if it were too awful a word for him to mention; yet hear what he says, "What if God willing to show his wrath, and to make his power known, endured with much long-suffering the vessels of wrath fitted to destruction" (Rom. 9:22). "For many walk, of whom I have told you often, and now tell you, even weeping, that they are the enemies of the cross of Christ: whose end is destruction" (Phil. 3:18–19). "For when they shall say, peace and safety, then sudden destruction cometh upon them" (1 Thess. 5:3). "The Lord Jesus shall be revealed from heaven, with his mighty angels, in flaming fire, taking vengeance on them that know not God, and that obey not the gospel of our Lord Jesus Christ, who shall be punished with everlasting destruction from the presence of the Lord, and from the glory of his power" (2 Thess. 1:7–9). Do not these show you, brethren, that they that have most love in their hearts speak most of hell?

The next person I would speak of is *John*, the beloved disciple. He had leaned on Jesus' bosom at the Last Supper, and drawn love out of His bosom. His character was love. You will notice how affectionately his epistles are written. He addresses them "beloved," "little children." Yet he speaks of hell; he calls it, seven times over, "the bottomless pit"— the pit where sinners shall sink through all eternity. He calls it the great wine press of the wrath of God (Rev. 14:19). But John has got another name for hell, "the lake of fire" (Rev. 20:14). It had often been called "hell"; but it was left for John, the beloved disciple, to call it "the lake of fire."

The next person I shall mention is *the Lord Jesus* Himself. Although He came from God, and "God is love," though He came to pluck brands from the burning, yet He speaks of hell. Though His mouth was most sweet, and His lips like lilies, dropping sweet-smelling myrrh—though "the Lord God had given Him the tongue of the learned, that He should know how to speak a word in season to him that is weary"; though He spoke as never man spoke—yet He spoke of hell. Hear what He says, "Whosoever shall say, thou fool, shall be in danger of hell fire" (Matt. 5:22). But I think the most awful words that ever came from His lips were, "Ye serpents, ye generation of vipers, how can ye escape the damnation of hell?" (Matt. 23:33). Again, "Depart from me, ye cursed, into everlasting fire" (Matt. 25:41). And He speaks of it in some of His parables too: "The angels shall come forth and sever the wicked from among the just, and shall cast them into the furnace of fire; there shall be wailing and gnashing of teeth" (Matt. 13:49–50). And He repeats the words of our text three times over. And could anything be plainer than the words in Mark: "He that believeth not shall be damned."

2. Why These Persons Speak So Plainly of Hell

These persons speak so plainly of hell *because it is all true*. Christ is the faithful and true witness. Once He said, "If it were not so, I would have told you." Once He said to Pilate "Every one that is of the truth heareth my voice." He Himself is "the truth." "It is impossible for God to lie." When Jesus appeared on earth, He came with love; He came to tell sinners of hell, and of a Savior to save them from hell; and how could He keep it back? He saw into hell, and how could He not speak of it? He was the faithful witness; so it was with David, Paul, and John. Paul said he had kept nothing back—he had not shunned to declare all the counsel of God. Now, how could he have said that, if he had not spoken of hell as he did? So must ministers. Suppose I never were to mention hell again, would that make it less tolerable? Oh, it is true! It is true! It is all true! And we cannot but mention it.

A second reason why they spoke so much of hell was *because they were full of love to sinners*. They are the best friends that do not flatter us. You know, beloved, Christ's bosom flowed with love. Out of love He had no where to lay His head; out of love He came to die; out of love, with tears He said, "O Jerusalem, Jerusalem, thou that killest the prophets, and stonest them which are sent unto thee, how often would I have gathered thy children together, even as a hen gathereth her chickens under her wings, and ye would not" (Matt. 23:37). And with the same breath He said, "How can we escape the damnation of hell?" So it was with Paul: "Knowing, therefore, the terror of the Lord we persuade men" (2 Cor. 5:11). Paul could weep over sinners; he says, "For many walk of whom I have told you often, and now tell you, even weeping, that they are the enemies of the cross of Christ" (Phil. 3:18). His tears fell on the parchment as he wrote. Oh! if we had more love to you, we would tell you more about hell. They do not love you that do not warn you, poor hell-deserving sinners. Oh! remember that love warns.

A third reason why they spoke so plainly of hell was *that they might be free from bloodguiltiness*. Jesus did not want your blood laid at His door, therefore He spoke of the "furnace of fire," and of the "worm that dieth not." Ah! He says, "How often would I have gathered you, but you would not!" God would not have bloodguiltiness laid to His charge. He says, "As I live, saith the Lord God, I have no pleasure in the death of the wicked; but that the wicked turn from his way and live. Turn ye, turn ye from your evil way, for why will ye die?" So it was with David, "Deliver me from bloodguiltiness, O God!" (Ps. 51:14). It was fear of bloodguiltiness that made David speak so plainly. So it was with Paul; he says, "I take you to record this day, that I am pure from the blood of all men" (Acts 20:26). So it is with ministers—we must acquit our consciences, and if you go to the judgment seat unpardoned, unsaved, your blood will be upon your own heads. As I was walking in the fields yesterday, that thought came with overwhelming power into my mind, that everyone I preached to would soon stand before the judgment seat, and be sent either to heaven or hell. Therefore, brethren, I must warn you, I must tell you about hell.

3. The Names Given to Hell

Let us consider the names given to hell in the Word of God. And the first is *fire*; it is taken from an earthly element suited to our capacity, as Christ takes to Himself a name to suit us, as a shepherd, a door, a way, a rock, an apple tree, the Rose of Sharon, etc. So when God speaks of heaven, He calls it Paradise, a city which has foundations, golden streets, pearly gates. One of these names will not describe it, nor any of them; for eye has not seen, nor ear heard, neither has it entered into the heart of man to conceive the things God has prepared for them that love Him. So when God speaks of hell He calls it a furnace of fire, a bottomless pit, perdition. Now, one of these names will not do, but take them altogether, and you may conceive something of what hell is.

The first name given to hell is *fire*. On the southern side of Mount Zion there is a valley covered over with vines—it is the valley of Hinnom, where Manasseh made his children pass through the fire of Moloch. This is the name by which Christ calls it, "a valley of fire." And, again He calls it "a furnace of fire," the walls will be fire, it will be fire above and below, and fire all round about. Again it is called "a lake of fire." The idea is something like a furnace of fire; it will be enclosed with burning mountains of brass. There will be no breath of wind to pass over their faces; it will be flames of fire forever and ever. It is called "devouring fire." "Who among us shall dwell with the devouring fire" (Isa. 33:14). Compare this with Hebrews 12:29: "For our God is a consuming fire." It is the nature of fire to consume, so it is with the fire of hell; but it will never annihilate the damned. O! it is a fire that will never be quenched; even the burning volcanoes will cease to burn, and that sun now sweetly shining upon us will cease to burn, and that very fire that is to burn up the elements will be quenched; but this fire is never quenched.

Another name given to hell in the Word of God is *the prison*. So we learn that the multitudes that perished at the flood are shut up in this prison. Ah! sinner, if you are shut up in it you will never come out till you have paid the uttermost farthing; and that you will never do—the bars are the justice and holiness of God.

Another name given to hell is *the pit*. Ah! it is the bottomless pit, where you will sink forever and ever; it will be a continual sinking deeper and deeper every day. Ah! sinner, is it not time to begin and cry, "Deliver me out of the mire, and let me not sink"? "Let not the deep swallow me up, and let not the pit shut her mouth upon me"?

Another name given to hell in the Word of God is *a falling into the hands of God*: "It is a fearful thing to fall into the hands of the living God" (Heb. 10:31). "Can thine heart endure, or can thine hands be strong, in the days that I shall deal with thee?" (Ezek. 22:14). God will be your irreconcilable enemy, sinner. God, who takes no pleasure in the death of the sinner, but rather that he should live—that God, I say, will be your eternal enemy if you die Christless—if you will not believe—if you will not be saved. O! what will you do, poor sinner, when His wrath is kindled.

Another name given to hell is the *second death*. "And death and hell were cast into the lake of fire. This is the second death" (Rev. 20:14). This is the meaning of God's threatening to Adam: "In the day that thou eatest thereof thou shalt surely die." Perhaps you may have stood by the bed of a dying sinner, and you may have seen how he gasps for breath—his teeth clenched—his hands clasp the bedclothes—his breath turns fainter and fainter till it dies away. Ah! this is the first death: and is like the second death. Ah! the man would try to resist, but he finds it is in vain; he finds eternal hell begun, and God dealing with him, and he sinks into gloom and dark despair. This is the death sinners are to die, and yet never die.

Another name given to hell is *outer darkness*. Christ calls it outer darkness. "But the children of the kingdom shall be cast out into outer darkness" (Matt. 8:12). "Bind him hand and foot, and take him away, and cast him into outer darkness" (Matt. 22:13). You will see it also in 2 Peter 2:4: "God spared not the angels that sinned, but cast them down to hell, and delivered them into chains of darkness." Again, Jude, verse 13: "Wandering stars, to whom is reserved the blackness of darkness forever." O! my dear friends, this is hell—"the blackness of darkness," "outer darkness," "chains of darkness."

4. The Hell Spoken of in the Bible Is Not Annihilation

I come now to show you that the hell spoken of in the Bible is not annihilation. Some people think that though they are not saved, they will be annihilated. O! it is a lie; I will show you that:

A. First of all, *by the cries of the damned.* "And he cried, and said, Father Abraham, have mercy upon me—for I am tormented in this flame" (Luke 16:24). And, again, look at the words in Matthew 22:13, "There shall be weeping and gnashing of teeth." O! these plainly show us that it is no annihilation. In hell the multitudes will be bundled up together in the great harvest day. "Gather ye together first the tares, and bind them in bundles to burn them" (Matt. 13:30). There will be bundles of swearers—bundles of Sabbath-breakers—bundles of drunkards—bundles of hypocrites—bundles of parents and children; they will be witnesses of each other's damnation.

B. Hell will be no annihilation, when we consider that *there will be different degrees of suffering.* "It shall be more tolerable for Tyre and Sidon at the day of judgment than for you" (Matt. 11:22). And it is said, the Pharisees would receive "greater damnation." Every man is to be judged according to his works.

C. It will be no annihilation, if we consider *the fate of Judas.* "Woe unto that man by whom the Son of man is betrayed; it had been good for that man if he had not been born" (Matt. 20:24). Judas is wishing he had never been born. I have no doubt he wishes to die, but will never be able to die. So it will be with all here who shall go to hell—all unworthy communicants. Ah! I tell you, if you die Christless, you will wish you had never been born—you will wish you had never seen the green earth or the blue sky. Ah! you will wish you had never been. O! dear brethren, better never to have had a being, than to be in hell. Ah! there are many in hell today who are cursing the day they were born.

D. It will be no annihilation, for *it is an eternal hell.* Some weak and foolish men think and please their fancy with the thought that hell will burn out, and they will come to some place where they may bathe their weary souls. Ah! you try to make an agreement with hell; but if ever there come a time when the flame that torments your soul and body shall burn out, then Jesus would be a liar, for three times He repeats the words of our text, and says, it shall never be quenched. It is eternal, for it is spoken of in words never used but to denote eternity "And the smoke of their torment ascendeth up forever and ever" (Rev. 14:11). Ah! you see it is forever and ever. Again, "And the devil that deceiveth them was cast into the lake of fire and brimstone, where the beast and the false prophet are, and shall be tormented day and night forever and ever" (Rev. 20:10). Compare this with Revelation 4:9, "And when those beasts give glory and honor and thanks to him that sat on the throne, who liveth for ever and ever." So you see the torments of the damned are spoken of with the eternity of God. Ah! if ever there comes a time when God ceases to live, then they may cease to suffer. Again, the eternity of hell and the eternity of heaven are spoken of in the very same language. "And there shall be no night there; and they need no candle, neither light of the sun; for the Lord God giveth them light: and they shall reign for ever and ever" (Rev. 22:5). The same words that are used for the eternity of the saints are used for the eternity of the damned. "They shall be tormented for ever and ever." O! sinner, if ever there comes a time when the saints shall fall from their thrones, or the immortal crowns fall from their heads, then you may think to leave hell; but that will never, never be—it is an eternal hell, "forever and ever"; eternity will be never ending wrath, always wrath to come. O! that you were wise, that you understood this, that you would consider your latter end.

5. This Eternal Hell Is Closed In and Surrounded by the Attributes of God

I come now, last of all, to consider that this eternal hell is closed in and surrounded by the attributes of God. This I shall leave, God willing, to another occasion. I shall now apply this:

A. First of all, *to you that are believers*. Dear brothers and sisters, all this hell that I have described is what you and I deserved. We were over the lake of fire, but it was from this that Jesus saved us; He was in the prison for you and me—He drank every drop out of the cup of God's wrath for you and me; He died, the just for the unjust. O! beloved, how should we prize, love, and adore Jesus for what He has done for us. O! we will never, never know, till safe across Jordan, how our hell has been suffered for us—how our iniquity has been pardoned. But, O! beloved, think of hell. Have you no unconverted friends, who are treasuring up wrath against the day of wrath? O! have you no prayerless parent, no sister, nor brother? O! have you no compassion for them—no mercy's voice to win them?

B. *To you that are seeking Christ anxiously.* I know some of you are. Dear soul, what a mercy in God to awaken you to flee from this fiery furnace! O! what a mercy to be awakened to flee—to be in earnest. Ah! your unconverted friends will tell you there is no need of being so anxious. O! is there no need to flee from the wrath to come? O! learn, dear soul, how precious Christ is; He is a hiding place from the wind, and a covert from the tempest. All the things in the world are like a speck of dust, all is loss for Jesus—He is all in all—He is free to you beloved—take no rest till you can say, He is mine.

C. *To you that are unconverted.* Ah! you are fools and you think you are wise; but O! I beseech you, search the Scriptures. Do not take my word about an eternal hell; it is the testimony of God, when He spoke about it. O! if it be true—if there be a furnace of fire—if there be a second death—if it is not annihilation, but an eternal hell—O! is it reasonable to go on living in sin? You think you are wise—that you are no fanatic—that you are no hypocrite; but you will soon gnash your teeth in pain; it will come; and the bitterest thought will be that you heard about hell, and yet rejected Christ. O! then, turn, turn, why will you die? Amen.

The Eternity of Hell Torments

Jonathan Edwards (1703–1758) was a Congregational preacher, a theologian and a philosopher, possessing one of the greatest minds ever produced on the American continent. He graduated with highest honors from Yale in 1720, and in 1726 was ordained and served as co-pastor with his grandfather, Solomon Stoddard, in Northfield, Massachusetts. When Stoddard died in 1729, Edwards became sole pastor, a position he held until doctrinal disagreements with the church led to his resignation in 1750. He played a key role in The Great Awakening (1734–44) and is perhaps best known for his sermon "Sinners in the Hands of an Angry God."

This sermon is taken from *The Works of Jonathan Edwards*, Volume 2, published by Banner of Truth Trust in 1976.

Jonathan Edwards

11

THE ETERNITY OF HELL TORMENTS

These shall go away into everlasting punishment (Matthew 25:46).

IN THIS CHAPTER we have the most particular description of the day of judgment of any in the whole Bible. Christ here declares that when He shall hereafter sit on the throne of His glory the righteous and the wicked shall be set before Him, and separated one from the other, as a shepherd divides his sheep from the goats. Then we have an account how both will be judged according to their works; how the good works of the one and the evil works of the other will be rehearsed, and how the sentence shall be pronounced accordingly. We are told what the sentence will be on each, and then we have an account of the execution of the sentence on both. In the words of the text is the account of the execution of the sentence on the wicked or the ungodly; concerning which, it is to my purpose to observe two things:

1. The duration of the punishment on which they are here said to enter: it is called everlasting punishment.

2. The time of their entrance on this everlasting punishment; that is after the day of judgment, when all these things that are of a temporary continuance shall have come to an end, and even those of them that are most lasting—the frame of the world itself; the earth which is said to abide forever; the ancient mountains and everlasting hills; the sun, moon, and stars. When the heavens shall have waxed old like a garment, and as a vesture shall be changed, then shall be the time when the wicked shall enter on their punishment.

Doctrine—The misery of the wicked in hell will be absolutely eternal.

There are two opinions which I mean to oppose by this doctrine. One is that the eternal death with which wicked men are threatened in Scripture signifies no more than eternal annihilation: that God will punish their wickedness by eternally abolishing their beings.

The other opinion which I mean to oppose is that though the punishment of the wicked shall consist in sensible misery, yet it shall not be absolutely eternal, but only of a very long continuance.

Therefore to establish the doctrine in opposition to these different opinions, I shall undertake to show,

1. That it is not contrary to the divine perfections to inflict on wicked men a punishment that is absolutely eternal.
2. That the eternal death which God threatens is not annihilation, but an abiding sensible punishment or misery.
3. That this misery will not only continue for a very long time, but will be absolutely without end.
4. That various good ends will be obtained by the eternal punishment of the wicked.

1. Eternal Punishment and the Character of God

I am to show that it is not contrary to the divine perfections to inflict on wicked men a punishment that is absolutely eternal.

This is the sum of the objections usually made against this doctrine, that it is inconsistent with the justice, and especially with the mercy, of God. And some say, if it be strictly just, yet how can we suppose that a merciful God can bear eternally to torment His creatures.

A. I shall briefly show that it is not inconsistent with the justice of God to inflict an eternal punishment. To evince this, I shall use only one argument, that is, that sin is heinous enough to deserve such a punishment, and such a punishment is no more than proportionate to the evil or demerit of sin. If the evil of sin be infinite, as the punishment is, then it is manifest that the punishment is no more than proportionate to the sin punished, and is no more than sin deserves. And if the obligation to love, honor, and obey God be infinite, then sin which is the violation of this obligation is a violation of infinite obligation, and so is an infinite evil. Again, if God be infinitely worthy of love, honor, and obedience, then our obligation to love, and honor, and obey Him is infinitely great. So that God being infinitely glorious, or infinitely worthy of our love, honor, and obedience, our obligation to love, honor, and obey Him, and so to avoid all sin, is infinitely great. Again, our obligation to love, honor, and obey God being infinitely great, sin is the violation of infinite obligation, and so is an infinite evil. Once more, sin being an infinite evil, deserves an infinite punishment, an infinite punishment is no more than it deserves: therefore such punishment is just; which was the thing to be proved. There is no evading the force of this reasoning, but by denying that God, the sovereign of the universe, is infinitely glorious; which I presume none of my hearers will venture to do.

B. I am to show that it is not inconsistent with the mercy of God, to inflict an eternal punishment on wicked men. It is an unreasonable and unscriptural notion of the mercy of God that He is merciful in such a sense that He cannot bear that penal justice should be executed. This is to conceive of the mercy of God as a passion to which His nature is so subject that God is liable to be moved, and affected, and overcome by seeing a creature in misery, so that He cannot bear to see justice executed: which is a most unworthy and absurd notion of the mercy of God, and would, if true, argue great weakness. It would be a great defect, and not a perfection, in the sovereign and supreme Judge of the world, to be merciful in such a sense that He could not bear to have penal justice executed. It is a very unscriptural notion of the mercy of God. The Scriptures everywhere represent the mercy of God as free and sovereign, and not that the exercises of it are necessary, so that God cannot bear justice should take place. The Scriptures abundantly speak of it as the glory of the divine attribute of mercy, that it is free and sovereign in its exercises; and not that God cannot but deliver sinners from misery. This is a mean and most unworthy idea of the divine mercy.

It is most absurd also as it is contrary to plain fact. For if there be any meaning in the objection, this is supposed in it, that all misery of the creature, whether just or unjust, is in itself contrary to the nature of God. For if His mercy be of such a nature that a very great degree of misery, though just, is contrary to His nature, then it is only to add to the mercy, and then a less degree of misery is contrary to His nature; again to add further to it, and a still less degree of misery is contrary to His nature. And so the mercy of God being infinite, all misery must be contrary to His nature; which we see to be contrary to fact: for we see that God in His providence, does indeed inflict very great calamities on mankind even in this life.

However strong such kind of objections against the eternal misery of the wicked may seem to the carnal, senseless hearts of men, as though it were against God's justice and mercy, yet their seeming strength arises from a want of sense of the infinite evil, odiousness, and provocation there is in sin. Hence it seems to us not suitable that any poor creature should be the subject of such misery, because we have no sense of anything abominable and provoking in any creature answerable to it. If we had, then this infinite calamity would not seem unsuitable. For one thing would but appear answerable and proportionate to another, and so the mind would rest in it as fit and suitable, and no more than what is proper to be ordered by the just, holy, and good Governor of the world.

That this is so we may be convinced by this consideration, that when we hear or read of some horrid instances of cruelty, it may be to some poor innocent child, or some holy martyr—and their cruel persecutors, having no regard to their shrieks and cries, only sported themselves with their misery, and would not vouchsafe even to put an end to their lives—we have a sense of the evil of them, and they make a deep impression on our minds. Hence it seems just, every way fit and suitable, that God should inflict a very terrible punishment on persons who have perpetrated such wickedness. It seems no way disagreeable to any perfection of the Judge of the world; we can think of it without being at all shocked. The reason is that we have a sense of the evil of their conduct, and a sense of the proportion there is between the evil or demerit and the punishment.

Just so, if we saw a proportion between the evil of sin and eternal punishment, if we saw something in wicked men that would appear as hateful to us as eternal misery appears dreadful; something that should as much stir up indignation and detestation as eternal misery does terror; all objections against the doctrine would vanish at once. Though now it seem incredible; though when we hear of it and are so often told of it, we know not how to realize it; though when we hear of such a degree and duration of torments as are held forth in this doctrine, and think what eternity is, it is ready to seem impossible that such torments should be inflicted on poor feeble creatures by a Creator of infinite mercy; yet this arises principally from these two causes: First, it is so contrary to the depraved inclinations of mankind that they hate to believe it and cannot bear it should be true. Second, they see not the suitableness of eternal punishment to the evil of sin; they see not that it is more than proportionate to the demerit of sin.

Having thus shown that the eternal punishment of the wicked is not inconsistent with the divine perfections, I shall now proceed to show that it is so far from being inconsistent with the divine perfections that those perfections evidently require it; that is, they require that sin should have so great a punishment, either in the person who has committed it, or in a surety; and therefore with respect to those who believe not in a surety, and have no interest in Him, the divine perfections require that this punishment should be inflicted on them.

This appears, as it is not only not unsuitable that sin should be thus punished; but it is positively suitable, decent, and proper. If this be made to appear, that it is positively suitable that sin should be thus punished, then it will follow that the perfections of God require it; for certainly the perfections of God require what is proper to be done. The perfection and excellency of God require that to take place which is perfect, excellent, and proper in its own nature. But that sin should be punished eternally is such a thing; which appears by the following considerations:

1. It is suitable that God should infinitely hate sin and be an infinite enemy to it. Sin, as I have before shown, is

an infinite evil, and therefore is infinitely odious and detestable. It is proper that God should hate every evil, and hate it according to its odious and detestable nature. And sin being infinitely evil and odious, it is proper that God should hate it infinitely.

2. If infinite hatred of sin be suitable to the divine character, then the *expressions* of such hatred are also suitable to His character. Because that which is suitable to be, is suitable to be expressed; that which is lovely in itself, is lovely when it appears. If it be suitable that God should be an infinite enemy to sin, or that He should hate it infinitely, then it is suitable that He should *act* as such an enemy. If it be suitable that He should hate and have enmity against sin, then it is suitable for Him to express that hatred and enmity in that to which hatred and enmity by its own nature tends. But certainly hatred in its own nature tends to opposition, and to set itself against that which is hated, and to procure its evil and not its good: and that in proportion to the hatred. Great hatred naturally tends to the great evil, and infinite hatred to the infinite evil, of its object.

Whence it follows that if it be suitable that there should be infinite hatred of sin in God, as I have shown it is, it is suitable that He should execute an infinite punishment on it; and so the perfections of God require that He should punish sin with an infinite, or which is the same thing, with an eternal, punishment.

Thus we see not only the great objection against this doctrine answered, but the truth of the doctrine established by reason. I now proceed further to establish it by considering the remaining particulars under the doctrine.

2. Eternal Death Is Not Annihilation

That eternal death or punishment which God threatens to the wicked is not annihilation, but an abiding sensible punishment or misery. The truth of this proposition will appear by the following particulars:

A. The Scripture everywhere represents the punishment of the wicked as implying very extreme pains and sufferings; but a state of annihilation is no state of suffering at all. Persons annihilated have not sense or feeling of pain or pleasure, and much less do they feel that punishment which carries in it an *extreme* pain or suffering. They no more suffer to eternity than they did suffer from eternity.

B. It is agreeable both to Scripture and reason to suppose that the wicked will be punished in such a manner that they shall be sensible of the punishment they are under; that they should be sensible that now God has executed and fulfilled what He threatened, what they disregarded, and would not believe. They should know themselves that justice takes place upon them; that God vindicates that majesty which they despised; that God is not so despicable a being as they thought Him to be. They should be sensible for what they are punished while they are under the threatened punishment. It is reasonable that they should be sensible of their own guilt, and should remember their former opportunities and obligations, and should see their own folly and God's justice. If the punishment threatened be eternal annihilation, they will never know that it is inflicted; they will never know that God is just in their punishment, or that they have their deserts. And how is this agreeable to the Scriptures, in which God threatens that He will repay the wicked *to his face* (Deut. 7:10). And to that in Job 21:19–20: "God rewardeth him, and he shall know it; his eyes shall see his destruction, and he shall drink of the wrath of the Almighty." And to that in Ezekiel 22:21–22: "Yea, I will gather you, and blow upon you in the fire of my wrath, and ye shall be melted in the midst thereof. As silver is melted in the midst of the furnace; and ye shall know that I the Lord have poured out my fury upon you." And how is it agreeable to that expression so often annexed to the threatenings of God's wrath against wicked men, *And ye shall know that I am the Lord*?

C. The Scripture teaches that the wicked will suffer different *degrees* of torment, according to the different aggravations of their sins. "Whosoever is angry with his brother without a cause, shall be in danger of the judgment: and whosoever shall say to his brother, Raca, shall be in danger of the council: but whosoever shall say, Thou fool, shall be in danger of hell-fire" (Matt. 5:22). Here

Christ teaches us that the torments of wicked men will be different in different persons, according to the different degrees of their guilt. It shall be more tolerable for Sodom and Gomorrah, for Tyre and Sidon, than for the cities where most of Christ's mighty works were wrought. Again our Lord assures us that he that knoweth his Lord's will, and prepareth not himself, nor doth according to His will, shall be beaten with many stripes. But he that knoweth not, and committeth things worthy of stripes, shall be beaten with few stripes. These several passages of Scripture infallibly prove that there will be different degrees of punishment in hell; which is utterly inconsistent with the supposition that the punishment consists in *annihilation*, in which there can be no *degrees*.

D. The Scriptures are very express and abundant in this matter, that the eternal punishment of the wicked will consist in sensible misery and torment, and not in annihilation. What is said of Judas is worthy to be observed here, "It had been good for that man if he had not been born" (Matt. 26:24). This seems plainly to teach us that the punishment of the wicked is such that their existence, upon the whole, is worse than non-existence. But if their punishment consists merely in annihilation, this is not true. The wicked, in their punishment, are said to *weep, and wail, and gnash their teeth*; which implies not only real existence, but life, knowledge, and activity, and that they are in a very sensible and exquisite manner affected with their punishment (Isa. 33:14). Sinners in the state of their punishment are represented to dwell with everlasting burnings. But if they are only turned into nothing, where is the foundation for this representation? It is absurd to say that sinners will dwell with annihilation; for there is no dwelling in the case. It is also absurd to call annihilation a burning, which implies a state of existence, sensibility, and extreme pain, whereas in annihilation there is neither.

It is said that they shall be cast into a lake of fire and brimstone. How can this expression with any propriety be understood to mean a state of annihilation? Yea, they are expressly said to have no rest day nor night, but to be tormented with fire and brimstone forever and ever (Rev. 20:10). But annihilation is a state of rest, a state in which not the least torment can possibly be suffered. The rich man in hell lifted up his eyes being in torment, and saw Abraham afar off, and Lazarus in his bosom, and entered into a particular conversation with Abraham; all which proves that he was not annihilated.

The spirits of ungodly men before the resurrection are not in a state of annihilation, but in a state of misery; they are spirits in prison, as the apostle saith of them that were drowned in the flood (1 Peter 3:19). And this appears very plainly from the instance of the rich man before mentioned, if we consider him as representing the wicked in their separate state between death and the resurrection. But if the wicked even then are in a state of torment, much more will they be when they shall come to suffer that which is the proper punishment of their sins.

Annihilation is not so great a calamity but that some men have undoubtedly chosen it rather than a state of suffering even in this life. This was the case of Job, a good man. But if a good man in this world may suffer that which is worse than annihilation, doubtless the proper punishment of the wicked, in which God means to manifest His peculiar abhorrence of their wickedness, will be a calamity vastly greater still; and therefore cannot be annihilation. That must be a very mean and contemptible testimony of God's wrath toward those who have rebelled against His crown and dignity—broken His laws, and despised both His vengeance and His grace—which is not so great a calamity as some of His true children have suffered in life.

The eternal punishment of the wicked is said to be the *second death* (Rev. 20:14; 21:8). It is doubtless called the second death in reference to the death of the body; and as the death of the body is ordinarily attended with great pain and distress, so the like, or something vastly greater, is implied in calling the eternal punishment of the wicked the *second death*; and there would be no propriety in calling it so if it consisted merely in annihilation. And this second death wicked men will suffer; for it cannot be called the second death with respect to any other than men; it cannot be called so with respect to the devils, as they die no temporal death, which is the first death. In Revelation 2:11 it is said, "He that overcometh, shall not be hurt of the second death"; implying that all who do not overcome their lusts, but live in sin, shall suffer the second death.

Again, wicked men will suffer the same kind of death with the devils; as in Matthew 25:41, "Depart, ye cursed, into everlasting fire, prepared for the devil and his angels." Now the punishment of the devil is not annihilation, but torment: he therefore trembles for fear of it; not for fear of being annihilated—he would be glad of that. What he is afraid of is torment, as appears by Luke 8:28 where he cries out, and beseeches Christ, that he would not torment him before the time. And it is said in Revelation 20:10, "The devil that deceived them was cast into the lake of fire and brimstone, where the beast and the false prophet are, and shall be tormented day and night, forever and ever."

It is strange how men will go directly against so plain and full revelations of Scripture as to suppose, notwithstanding all these things, that the eternal punishment threatened against the wicked signifies no more than annihilation.

3. Punishment of the Wicked Will Never End

As the future punishment of the wicked consists in sensible misery; so it shall not only continue for a very long time, but shall be absolutely without end.

Of those who have held that the torments of hell are not absolutely eternal, there have been two sorts. Some suppose that in the threatenings of everlasting punishment the terms used do not necessarily import a proper eternity, but only a very long duration. Others suppose that if they do import a proper eternity, yet we cannot necessarily conclude thence, that God will fulfill His threatenings. Therefore I shall,

First, show that the threatenings of eternal punishment do very plainly and fully import a proper absolute eternity, and not merely a long duration.

A. This appears because when the Scripture speaks of the wicked being sentenced to their punishment at the time when all temporal things are come to an end, it then speaks of it as everlasting, as in the text, and elsewhere. It is true, that the term *forever* is not always in Scripture used to signify eternity. Sometimes it means, as long as a man lives. In this sense it is said that the Hebrew servant, who chose to abide with his master, should have his ear bored, and should serve his master forever. Sometimes it means, during the continuance of the state and church of the Jews. In this sense, several laws, which were peculiar to that church, and were to continue in force no longer than that church should last, are called "statutes forever" (see Ex. 27:21; 28:43, etc.). Sometimes it means as long as the world stands. "One generation passeth away, and another generation cometh; but the earth abideth forever" (Eccl. 1:4).

And this last is the longest temporal duration that such a term is ever used to signify. For the duration of the world is the longest of things temporal, as its beginning was the earliest. Therefore when the Scripture speaks of things as being before the foundation of the world, it means that they existed before the beginning of time. So those things which continue after the end of the world are eternal things. When heaven and earth are shaken and removed, those things that remain will be what cannot be shaken, but will remain forever (Heb. 12:26–27).

But the punishment of the wicked will not only remain after the end of the world, but is called everlasting, as in the text, "These shall go away into everlasting punishment." It is also stated as everlasting in 2 Thessalonians 1:9–10: "Who shall be punished with everlasting destruction from the presence of the Lord, and from the glory of his power: when he shall come to be glorified in his saints." Now, what can be meant by a thing being everlasting, *after* all temporal things are come to an end, but that it is absolutely without end?

B. Such expressions are used to set forth the duration of the punishment of the wicked as are never used in the Scriptures of the New Testament to signify anything but a proper eternity. It is said not only that the punishment shall be forever, but *forever and ever*. "The smoke of their torment ascendeth up *forever and ever*" (Rev. 14:11). "Shall be tormented day and night, *forever and ever*" (Rev. 20:10). Doubtless the New Testament has some expression to signify a proper eternity, of which it has so often occasion to speak. But it has no higher expression than this: if this does not signify an absolute eternity, there is none that does.

C. The Scripture uses the same way of speaking to set forth the eternity of *punishment* and the eternity of *happiness*, yea, the eternity of God Himself. "These shall go away into *everlasting* punishment: but the righteous into life *eternal*." The words *everlasting* and *eternal*, in the original, are the very same. "And they [the saints] shall reign *forever and ever*" (Rev. 22:5). And the Scripture has no higher expression to signify the eternity of God Himself, than that of His being *forever and ever*; as in Revelation 4:9, "To him who sat on the throne, who liveth forever and ever" (see also Rev. 4:10; 5:14; 10:6; 15:7).

Again, the Scripture expresses God's eternity by this, that it shall be *forever*, after the world is come to an end. "They shall perish, but thou shalt endure: yea, all of them shall wax old like a garment; as a vesture shalt thou change them, and they shall be changed. But thou art the same, and thy years shall have no end" (Ps. 102:26–27).

D. The Scripture says that wicked men shall not be delivered, till they have paid the uttermost farthing of their debt (Matt. 5:26). The last mite (Luke 10:59); that is, the utmost that is deserved; and all *mercy* is excluded by this expression. But we have shown that they *deserve* an infinite, an endless punishment.

E. The Scripture says absolutely that their punishment shall not have an end. "Where their worm dieth not, and the fire is not quenched" (Mark 9:44). Now, it will not do to say that the meaning is, their worm shall live a *great while*, or that it shall be a great while before their fire is quenched. If ever the time comes that their worm shall *die*; if ever there shall be a *quenching* of the fire at all, then it is not true that their worm *dies not*, and that the fire is *not quenched*. For if there be a dying of the worm, and a quenching of the fire, let it be at what time it will, nearer or further off, it is equally contrary to such a negation—*it dies not, it is not quenched.*

Secondly, there are others who allow that the expressions of the threatenings do denote a proper eternity; but then, they say, it does not certainly follow, that the punishment will really be eternal; because God may *threaten,* and yet not *fulfill* His threatenings. Though they allow that the threatenings are positive and peremptory, without any reserve, yet they say, God is not obliged to fulfill absolute positive threatenings, as He is absolute promises. Because in promises a right is conveyed that the creature to whom the promises are made will claim; but there is no danger of the creature's claiming any right by a threatening. Therefore I am now to show that what God has positively declared in this matter, does indeed make it certain that it shall be as He has declared. To this end I shall motion two things:

A. It is evidently contrary to the divine *truth*, positively to declare anything to be real, whether past, present, or to come, which God at the same time knows is not so. Absolutely threatening that anything shall be is the same as absolutely declaring that it is to be. For any to suppose that God absolutely declares that anything *will be*, which He at the same time knows *will not be*, is blasphemy, if there be any such thing as blasphemy.

Indeed, it is very true that there is no *obligation* on God arising from the claim of the creature, as there is in promises. They seem to reckon the wrong way, who suppose the necessity of the execution of the threatening to arise from a proper obligation on God to the creature to execute consequent on His threatening. For indeed the certainty of the execution arises the other way, that is, on the obligation there was on the omniscient God, in threatening, to conform His threatening to what He knew would be future in execution. Though, strictly speaking, God is not properly *obliged* to the creature to execute because He has threatened, yet He was obliged not *absolutely* to threaten, if at the same time He knew that He should not or would not fulfill: because this would not have been consistent with His truth. So that from the truth of God there is an inviolable connection between positive threatenings and execution. They who suppose that God positively declared that He would do contrary to what He knew would come to pass, do therein suppose that He absolutely threatened contrary to what He knew to be *truth*. And how anyone can speak contrary to what He knows to be truth, in declaring, promising, or threatening, or any other way, consistently with inviolable truth, is inconceivable.

Threatenings are significations of something; and if they are made consistently with truth, they are true significations, or significations of truth, *that which shall be*. If absolute threatenings are significations of the *futurity* of the things threatened. But if the futurity of the things threatened be not true and real, then how can the threatening be a *true* signification? And if God, in them, speaks contrary to what He *knows* and contrary to what He *intends*, how He can speak true is inconceivable.

Absolute threatenings are a kind of *predictions*; and though God is not properly *obliged* by any claim of ours to fulfill predictions, unless they are of the nature of promises, yet it certainly would be contrary to *truth* to predict that such a thing would come to pass. Threatenings are declarations of something future, and they must be declarations of future truth, if they are true declarations. Its being future alters not the case anymore than if it were present. It is equally contrary to truth to declare contrary to what at the same time is known to be truth, whether it be of things past, present, or to come; for all are alike to God.

Beside, we have often declarations in Scripture of the future eternal punishment of the wicked in the proper form of *predictions*, and not in the form of *threatenings*. So in the text, "These shall go away into everlasting punishment." So in those frequent assertions of eternal punishment in the Revelation, some of which I have already quoted. The Revelation is a *prophecy*, and is so called in the book itself; so are those declarations of eternal punishment. The like declarations we have also in many other places of Scripture.

B. The doctrine of those who teach that it is not certain that God will fulfill those absolute threatenings is *blasphemous* another way; and that is as God, according to their supposition, was obliged to make use of a *fallacy* to govern the world. They own that it is needful that men should *apprehend* themselves liable to an eternal punishment that they might thereby be restrained from sin, and that God has threatened such a punishment for the very end that they might *believe* themselves exposed to it. But what an unworthy opinion does this convey of God and His government, of His infinite majesty, and wisdom, and all-sufficiency! Besides, they suppose that though God has made use of such a fallacy, yet it is not such an one but that they have *detected* Him in it. Though God *intended* men should believe it to be certain that sinners are liable to an eternal punishment, yet they suppose that they have been so cunning as to find out that it is not certain: and so that God had not laid His design so deep but that such cunning men as they can discern the cheat, and defeat the design: because they have found out that there is no necessary connection between the threatening of eternal punishment, and the execution of that threatening.

Considering these things, is it not greatly to be wondered at that Archbishop Tillotson, who has made so great a figure among the new-fashioned divines, should advance such an opinion as this?

Objections Answered

Before I conclude this head, it may be proper for me to answer an objection or two that may arise in the minds of some.

1. It may be here said we have instances wherein God has not fulfilled His threatenings; as His threatening to Adam, and in him to mankind, that they should surely die, if they should eat the forbidden fruit. I answer, it is not true that God did not fulfill that threatening: He fulfilled it, and will fulfill it in every jot and tittle. When

God said, "Thou shalt surely die," if we respect spiritual death, it was fulfilled in Adam's person in the day that he ate. For immediately His image, His holy spirit, and original righteousness, which was the highest and best life of our first parents, were lost; and they were immediately in a doleful state of spiritual death.

If we respect temporal death, that was also fulfilled: he brought death upon himself and all his posterity, and he virtually suffered that death on that very day on which he ate. His body was brought into a corruptible, mortal, and dying condition, and so it continued till it was dissolved. If we look at all that death which was comprehended in the threatening, it was, properly speaking, fulfilled in Christ. When God said to Adam, "If thou eatest, thou shalt die," He spoke not only to him, and of him personally; but the words respected mankind, Adam and his race, and doubtless were so understood by him. His offspring were to be looked upon as sinning in him, and so should die with him. The words do as justly allow of an imputation of death as of sin; they are as well consistent with *dying* in a surety, as with *sinning* in one. Therefore, the threatening is fulfilled in the death of Christ, the surety.

2. Another objection may arise from God's threatening to Nineveh. He threatened that in forty days Nineveh should be destroyed, which yet He did not fulfill. I answer, that threatening could justly be looked upon no otherwise than as *conditional*. It was of the nature of a *warning*, and not of an absolute denunciation. Why was Jonah sent to the Ninevites, but to give them warning that they might have opportunity to repent, reform, and avert the approaching destruction? God had no other design or end in sending the prophet to them, but that they might be warned and tried by him, as God warned the Israelites, Judah and Jerusalem, before their destruction. Therefore the prophets, together with their prophecies of approaching destruction, joined earnest exhortations to repent and reform, that it might be averted.

No more could justly be understood to be certainly threatened than that Nineveh should be destroyed in forty days, *continuing as it was*. For it was for their wickedness that that destruction was threatened, and so the Ninevites took it. Therefore, when the cause was removed, the effect ceased. It was contrary to God's known manner to threaten punishment and destruction for sin in this world absolutely, so that it should come upon the persons threatened unavoidably, let them repent and reform and do what they would: "At what instant I shall speak concerning a nation, and concerning a kingdom, to pluck up, and to pull down, and to destroy it; if that nation against whom I have pronounced turn from their evil, I will repent of the evil that I thought to do unto them" (Jer. 18:7–8). So that all threatenings of this nature had a *condition* implied in them, according to the known and declared manner of God's dealing. And the Ninevites did not take it as an *absolute* sentence of denunciation: if they had, they would have despaired of any benefit by fasting and reformation.

But the threatenings of eternal wrath are positive and absolute. There is nothing in the Word of God from which we can gather any condition. The only opportunity of escaping is in this world; this is the only state of trial, wherein we have any offers of mercy, or place for repentance.

Eternal Punishment Accomplishes Good

I shall mention several good and important *ends*, which will be obtained by the eternal punishment of the wicked.

A. Hereby God vindicates His injured *majesty*. Wherein sinners cast contempt upon it, and trample it in the dust, God vindicates and honors it, and makes it appear, as it is indeed, infinite, by showing that it is infinitely dreadful to contemn or offend it.

B. God glorifies His *justice*. The glory of God is the greatest good; it is that which is the chief end of the creation; it is of greater importance than anything else. But this is one way wherein God will glorify Himself, as in the eternal destruction of ungodly men He will glorify His justice. Therein He will appear as a just governor of the world. The vindictive justice of God will appear strict, exact, awful, and terrible, and therefore glorious.

C. God hereby indirectly glorifies His *grace* on the

vessels of mercy. The saints in heaven will behold the torments of the damned: "the smoke of their torment ascendeth up forever and ever." "And they shall go forth and look upon the carcasses of the men that have transgressed against me: for their worm shall not die, neither shall their fire be quenched, and they shall be an abhorring unto flesh" (Isa. 66:24). And in Revelation 14:10 it is said that they shall be tormented in the presence of the holy angels, and in the presence of the Lamb. So they will be tormented in the presence also of the glorified saints.

Hereby the saints will be made the more sensible how great their salvation is. When they shall see how great the misery is from which God has saved them, and how great a difference He has made between their state, and the state of others, who were by nature, and perhaps for a time by practice, no more sinful and ill-deserving than any, it will give them a greater sense of the wonderfulness of God's grace to them. Every time they look upon the damned, it will excite in them a lively and admiring sense of the grace of God, in making them so to differ. This the apostle informs us is one end of the damnation of ungodly men. "What if God willing to show his wrath, and to make his power known, endured with much longsuffering the vessels of wrath fitted to destruction: and that he might make known *the riches of his glory on the vessels of mercy*, which he had afore prepared unto glory?" (Rom. 9:22–23). The view of the misery of the damned will double the ardor of the love and gratitude of the saints in heaven.

D. The sight of hell torments will exalt the *happiness of the saints* forever. It will not only make them more sensible of the greatness and freeness of the grace of God in their happiness, but it will really make their happiness the greater as it will make them more sensible of their own happiness; it will give them a more lively relish of it; it will make them prize it more. When they see others, who were of the same nature, and born under the same circumstances, plunged in such misery, and they so distinguished, O it will make them sensible how happy they are. A sense of the opposite misery, in all cases, greatly increases the relish of any joy or pleasure.

The sight of the wonderful power, the great and dreadful majesty, and awful justice and holiness of God, manifested in the eternal punishment of ungodly men, will make them prize His favor and love vastly the more; and they will be so much the more happy in the enjoyment of it.

Application

1. From what has been said, we may learn the folly and madness of the greater part of mankind, in that for the sake of present momentary gratification, they run the venture of enduring all these eternal torments. They prefer a small pleasure, or a little wealth, or a little earthly honor and greatness, which can last but for a moment, to an escape from this punishment. If it be true that the torments of hell are eternal, what will it profit a man, if he gain the whole world and lose his own soul; or what shall a man give in exchange for his soul? What is there in this world which is not a trifle, and lighter than vanity, in comparison with these eternal things?

How mad are men who so often hear of these things and pretend to believe them; who can live but a little while, a few years; who do not even expect to live here longer than others of their species ordinarily do; and who yet are careless about what becomes of themselves in another world, where there is no change and no end! How mad are they, when they hear that if they go on in sin, they shall be eternally miserable, that they are not moved by it, but hear it with as much carelessness and coldness as if they were no way concerned in the matter; when they know not but that it may be their case that they may be suffering these torments before a week is at an end!

How can men be so careless of such a matter as their own eternal and desperate destruction and torment! What a strange stupor and senselessness possesses the hearts of men! How common a thing is it to see men, who are told from Sabbath to Sabbath of eternal misery, and who are as mortal as other men, so careless about it that they seem not to be at all restrained by it from whatever their souls lust after! It is not half so much their care to escape eternal misery as it is to get money and land, and to be considerable in the world, and to gratify their senses. Their thoughts are much more exercised about these things, and much more of their care and concern is about them. Eternal misery, though they lie every day exposed to it, is a thing neglected; it is but now and then thought of, and then with a great deal of stupidity, and not with concern enough to stir them up to do anything considerable in order to escape it. They are not sensible that it is worth their while to take any considerable pains in order to avoid it. And if they do take pains for a little while, they soon leave off, and something else takes up their thoughts and concern.

Thus you see it among young and old. Multitudes of youth lead careless lives, taking little care about their salvation. So you may see it among persons of middle age, and with many advanced in years, and when they certainly draw near to the grave. Yet these same persons will seem to acknowledge that the greater part of men go to hell and suffer eternal misery, and this through carelessness about it. However, they will do the same. How strange is it that men can enjoy themselves and be at rest when they are thus hanging over eternal burnings; at the same time, having no lease of their lives, and not knowing how soon the thread by which they hang will break, nor indeed do they pretend to know; and if it breaks, they are gone, they are lost forever, and there is no remedy! Yet they trouble not themselves much about it; nor will they hearken to those who cry to them and entreat them to take care for themselves, and labor to get out of that dangerous condition: they are not willing to take so much pains: they choose not to be diverted from amusing themselves with toys and vanities. Thus, well might the wise man say, "The heart of the sons of men is full of evil. Madness is in their heart while they live; and after that they go to the dead" (Eccl. 9:3). How much wiser are those few who make it their main business to lay a foundation for eternity, to secure their salvation!

2. I shall improve this subject in a use of exhortation to sinners to take care to escape these eternal torments. If they be eternal, one could think that would be enough to awaken your concern, and excite your diligence. If the punishment be eternal, it is infinite, as we said before; and therefore no other evil, no death, no temporary torment that ever you heard of, or that you can imagine, is anything in comparison with it, but is as much less and less considerable, not only as a grain of sand is less than the whole universe, but as it is less than the boundless space which encompasses the universe. Therefore:

a. Be entreated to consider attentively how great and awful a thing eternity is. Although you cannot comprehend it the more by considering, yet you may be made more sensible that it is not a thing to be disregarded. Do but consider what it is to suffer extreme torment forever and ever; to suffer it day and night, from one year to another, from one age to another, and from one thousand ages to another, and so adding age to age, and thousands to thousands, in pain, in wailing and lamenting, groaning and shrieking, and gnashing your teeth; with your souls full of dreadful grief and amazement, with your bodies and every member full of racking torture, without any possibility of getting ease; without any possibility of moving God to pity by your cries; without any possibility of hiding yourselves from Him; without any possibility of diverting your thoughts from your pain; without any possibility of obtaining any manner of mitigation, or help, or change for the better.

b. Do but consider how dreadful despair will be in such torment. How dismal will it be when you are under these racking torments, to know assuredly that you never, never shall be delivered from them; to have no hope: when you shall wish that you might be turned into nothing, but shall have no hope of it; when you shall wish that you might be turned into a toad or a serpent, but shall have not hope of it; when you would rejoice, if you might but have any relief, after you shall have endured these torments millions of ages, but shall have no hope of it. After you shall have worn out the age of the sun, moon, and stars, in your dolorous groans and lamentations, without rest day and night, or one minute's ease, yet you shall have no hope of ever being delivered; after you shall have worn a thousand more such ages, you shall have no hope, but shall know that you are not one whit nearer to the end of your torments; but that still there are the same groans, the same shrieks, the same doleful cries, incessantly to be made by you, and that the smoke of your torment shall still ascend up forever and ever. Your souls, which shall have been agitated with the wrath of God all this while, will still exist to bear more wrath; your bodies, which shall have been burning all this while in these glowing flames, shall not have been consumed, but will remain to roast through eternity, which will not have been at all shortened by what shall have been past.

You may by considering make yourselves more sensible than you ordinarily are; but it is little you can conceive of what it is to have no hope in such torments. How sinking would it be to you to endure such pain as you have felt in this world, without any hopes, and to know that you never should be delivered from it, nor have one minute's rest! You can now scarcely conceive how doleful that would be. How much more to endure the vast weight of the wrath of God without hope! The more the damned in hell think of the eternity of their torments, the more amazing will it appear to them; and alas! They will not be able to keep it out of their minds. Their tortures will not divert them from it, but will fix their attention to it. O how dreadful will eternity appear to them after they shall have been thinking on it for ages together, and shall have so long an experience of their torments! The damned in hell will have two infinities perpetually to amaze them, and swallow them up: one is an infinite God, whose wrath they will bear, and in whom they will behold their perfect and irreconcilable enemy. The other is the infinite duration of their torment.

If it were possible for the damned in hell to have a comprehensive knowledge of eternity, their sorrow and grief would be infinite in degree. The comprehensive view of so much sorrow which they must endure, would cause infinite grief for the present. Though they will not have a comprehensive knowledge of it, yet they will doubtless have a vastly more lively and strong apprehension of it than we can have in this world. Their torments will give them an impression of it. A man in his present state, without any enlargement of his capacity, would have a vastly more lively impression of eternity than he has if he were only under some pretty sharp pain in some member of his body, and were at the same time assured that he must endure that pain forever. His pain would give him a greater sense of eternity than other men have. How much more will those excruciating torments which the damned will suffer, have this effect!

Besides, their capacity will probably be enlarged, their understandings will be quicker and stronger in a future state; and God can give them as great a sense and as strong an impression of eternity as He pleases to increase their grief and torment. O be entreated, you that are in a Christless state, and are going on in a way to hell, that are daily exposed to damnation, to consider these things. If you do not, it will surely be but a little while before you will experience them, and then you will know how dreadful it is to despair in hell; and it may be before this year, or this month, or this week, is at an end; before another Sabbath, or ever you shall have opportunity to hear another sermon.

c. That you may effectually escape these dreadful and eternal torments, be entreated to flee and embrace Him who came into the world for the very end of saving sinners from these torments, who has paid the whole debt due to the divine law, and exhausted eternal in temporal sufferings. What great encouragement is it to those of you who are sensible that you are exposed to eternal punishment that there is a Savior provided, who is able and who freely offers to save you from that punishment, and that in a way which is perfectly consistent with the glory of God, yea, which is more to the glory of God than it would be if you should suffer the eternal punishment of hell. For if you should suffer that punishment you would never pay the whole of the debt. Those who are sent to hell never will have paid the whole of the debt which they owe to God, nor indeed a part which bears any proportion to the whole. They never will have paid a part which bears so great a proportion to the whole as one mite to ten thousand talents. Justice therefore never can be actually satisfied in your damnation; but it is actually satisfied in Christ. Therefore He is accepted of the Father, and therefore all who believe are accepted and justified in Him. Therefore believe in Him, come to Him, commit your souls to Him to be saved by Him. In Him you shall be safe from the eternal torments of hell. Nor is that all: but through Him you shall inherit inconceivable blessedness and glory, which will be of equal duration with the torments of hell. For, as at the last day the wicked shall go away into *everlasting* punishment, so shall the righteous, or those who trust in Christ, go into life *eternal.*